HARMONY

DEVEL(and)PMENT

ASEAN–China Relations

HARMONY
DEVEL(and)OPMENT
ASEAN–China Relations

Editors

Lai Hongyi
Lim Tin Seng

East Asian Institute, National University of Singapore

World Scientific

NEW JERSEY · LONDON · SINGAPORE · BEIJING · SHANGHAI · HONG KONG · TAIPEI · CHENNAI

Published by

World Scientific Publishing Co. Pte. Ltd.

5 Toh Tuck Link, Singapore 596224

USA office: 27 Warren Street, Suite 401-402, Hackensack, NJ 07601

UK office: 57 Shelton Street, Covent Garden, London WC2H 9HE

British Library Cataloguing-in-Publication Data
A catalogue record for this book is available from the British Library.

HARMONY AND DEVELOPMENT: ASEAN–CHINA RELATIONS

ISBN-13 978-981-270-970-7
ISBN-10 981-270-970-3
ISBN-13 978-981-270-971-4 (pbk)
ISBN-10 981-270-971-1 (pbk)

Printed by FuIsland Offset Printing (S) Pte Ltd, Singapore

Contents

Acknowledgements

The publication of this volume has received considerable help from several individuals. Professor John WONG, the Research Director of East Asian Institute (EAI), National University of Singapore, was a key person in organising the symposium from which this volume is based. He also delegated the editing task to us and offered helpful comments. LIAN Wee Li and James TAN, along with a few EAI administrative staff members, took care of the administrative part of the conference while Jessica LOON, Senior Research Officer at EAI, did a timely and conscientious job in copy-editing the volume. Here we thank them for their help and assistance which make the timely publication of this volume possible.

About the Editors and Contributors

Editors

LAI Hongyi is Senior Research Fellow at East Asian Institute (EAI), National University of Singapore. He obtained his B.A. in international politics from Beijing University, and M.A. and Ph.D. in political science from the University of California at Los Angeles. His research covers China's political economy and external policies. He has published book chapters in English on China's anti-epidemic cooperation with Southeast Asia and on China's studies of Southeast Asia. His books in English include *Reform and the Non-State Economy in China — The Political Economy of Liberalization Strategies* (Palgrave MacMillan, 2006) and *China into the Hu-Wen Era* (World Scientific, 2006). He also has three published and forthcoming books in English. In addition, he has 15 published articles in refereed journals, including leading area studies journals such as *China Journal, Modern China,* and *Third World Quarterly*. His publications in Chinese include published and forthcoming books and 11 academic journal articles and book chapters.

LIM Tin Seng is a research officer at the East Asian Institute, Singapore. He received his M.A. in History from the National University of Singapore. His research focuses on China's foreign relations with developing countries as well as the history of Singapore. He is the author of "Seeking Closer Cooperation with Post-Suharto Indonesia" and co-authored "Malaysia's Relations with China: From Mahathir to Badawi" and "China's Growing Influence in Africa" in *Interpreting China's Development* (World Scientific, 2007).

Contributors

GAN Kim Yong is a Member of Parliament and currently the Minister of State (Ministry of Education and Ministry of Manpower, Singapore). He obtained his M.A. from Cambridge University. He has served as Assistant Director and Deputy Director at the Ministry of Trade & Industry, Head of Research at the Ministry of Home Affairs, as well as Manager, Senior Manager, and CEO and President of NatSteel Ltd.

ONG Keng Yong is Secretary-General of ASEAN. He joined the Singapore Ministry of Foreign Affairs in 1979 and held senior positions including director in charge of American and European affairs, Singapore's High Commissioner to India and ambassador to Nepal. He was seconded to Singapore Prime Minister's Office as the press secretary to the Prime Minister and concurrently to the Ministry of Information, Communications and the Arts as deputy secretary.

Jusuf WANANDI is a senior fellow at the Centre for Strategic and International Studies (CSIS), and Vice Chair of the Board of Trustees of CSIS Foundation. He is also Chairman of the Indonesian National Committee for Pacific Economic Cooperation Council (PECC) and Chairman of CSCAP Indonesia and President Director of the *Jakarta Post*. His research focuses on political and security developments in the Asia Pacific region and Indonesian foreign affairs. Jusuf Wanandi was Assistant Professor of Law at the University of Indonesia. He was appointed as Secretary of the Indonesian Supreme Advisory Council, Secretary General of the National Education Council, and as four-term representative in the People's Consultative Assembly. His recent publications include *Global, Regional and National: Strategic Issues and Linkages* (2006).

SHENG Lijun is a senior fellow at the Institute of Southeast Asian Studies, Singapore. He received his PhD from the University of Queensland. His research focuses on China's foreign relations in East Asia. He has written extensively, with articles published in numerous journals including the *Washington Quarterly*, the *Journal of Strategic Studies, Cambridge Review of International Affairs, Security Dialogue,*

Asian Perspective, Journal of Northeast Asian Studies, Contemporary Southeast Asia, and *Pacific Focus.* He was the co-editor of *Chinese Political, Economical and Social Overview of Vietnam* (2006) and *ASEAN-China Relations: Realities and Prospects* (2006).

LI Chenyang is Associate Researcher and Executive Vice Director of the Institute of Southeast Asian Studies at the School of International Relations of Yunnan University. He is also a member of the executive council of China's Society of Southeast Asian Studies. He received his B.A. in the Myanmarese language from the PLA Foreign Languages College in 1991 and M.A. from Beijing University in 1996. He is a joint author of six scholarly works including *A Study of Myanmar (Miandian yanjiu)* (Junshi yiwen chubanshe, 2001) and *An Overview of the Military of Member States of ASEAN (Dongmeng geguo junqing gailan)* (Junshi yiwen chubanshe, 2003).

Ignatius Wibowo WIBISONO is Head of the Centre of Chinese Studies, Jakarta and Lecturer at the University of Indonesia. He received his PhD in Chinese politics from the University of London and M.A. from Marquette University. His research focuses on Indonesia's relations with China. He has published many books and numerous articles in reputable journals.

DO Tien Sam is Director and Associate Professor of the Centre for ASEAN and China Studies, Vietnam Academy of Social Sciences.

WANG Yan is currently the Vice Chair and Associate Professor of the English Department of China Foreign Affairs University (*waijiao xueyuan*) in Beijing, China. She graduated from Beijing Foreign Languages University in 1980. She obtained her M.A. in international relations from the Fletcher School (of law and diplomacy), Tufts University in 1987. As a Fulbright Scholar she visited and researched at the University of Virginia from 1996–1997. From 1998 to 1999 she also jointly chaired a seminar on China-US negotiations and conflict management at the Law School of Harvard University. She teaches translation, negotiations and political treatise.

ZHANG Zhenjiang is the Deputy Director of Institute of Southeast Asian Studies and Vice Dean of the Department of International Relations, Jinan University, Guangzhou, China. He obtained his PhD from Nanjing University. His research interests cover theory and history of international relations, American diplomatic history, international relations in Asia-Pacific, ASEAN regionalism. His published monographs include *The Cold War and the Civil War: US-Soviet Struggle for Power and the Origin of the Chinese Civil War, 1944–1945* (2005) (in Chinese) and *From Sterling to US Dollar: Transition of the International Economic Hegemony, 1933–1945* (2006) (in Chinese).

Bounnheuang SONGNAVONG is Deputy Director-General of the Institute of Foreign Affairs, Ministry of Foreign Affairs, Lao People's Democratic Republic.

Aung Kyaw Oo is Director of Myanmar Institute of Strategic and International Studies, Ministry of Foreign Affairs, Yangon, Myanmar.

LU Jianren is professor at the Institute of Asia-Pacific Studies, Chinese Academy of Social Sciences, China. He received his PhD in Economics from the People's University of China. His research focuses on Asia-Pacific economic relations.

ZHAO Hong is an associate professor at the Research School of Southeast Asian Studies, Xiamen University. He obtained his PhD in economics from Xiamen University. He is the author of *The History, Current Status and Development Trend of Sino-ASEAN Economic and Trade Relations Under the Background of Globalization* (co-author, 2006, in Chinese) and co-author of *A Study of the Financial Development in Malaysia* (2005, in Chinese). His recent article appeared in *Contemporary Southeast Asia*. His research interests are on China-ASEAN economic integration and East Asian economic community.

TENG Siow Song is a research officer at the East Asian Institute, Singapore. He received his M.A. in Economics from the University of Sydney. His research focuses on ASEAN-China trade and economic relations. Prior to joining the academia, he worked in the private sector and was based in China and Vietnam.

LIAO Shaolian is Deputy Director and professor at the Centre for Southeast Asian Studies, Xiamen University, China. He is also Vice President of China Association of Southeast Asian Studies. He was educated in Zhongshan University in the 1960s, and later studied world economy at Fudan University and development economics at Cornell University in the early 1980s. He authored four books and more than 70 articles on economic development and cooperation in Southeast Asia and the Asia Pacific region.

Stephen LEONG is assistant Director-General at the Institute of Strategic and International Studies (ISIS) Malaysia. He received his PhD from UCLA and had a long academic career with the University of Malaya. He is also Co-Director of ISIS Malaysia's Centre for International Dialogue; Director-General of the Malaysian National Committee for Pacific Economic Cooperation (MANCPEC); Secretary-General, Network for East Asian Think-tanks (NEAT) Malaysia. His recent publications include *Asia Pacific Security: Imperatives for Cooperation* (editor, 2006) and *Asia Pacific Security: Challenges and Opportunities in the 21st Century* (co-editor, 2002).

Ellen H. PALANCA is professor at the Department of Economics, Ateneo de Manila University, the Philippines. She is also Director of the Chinese Studies Programme at the School of Social Sciences and a board member of the Ateno Centre for Asian Studies. Her research focuses on China-Philippine relations. Her recent publications include *China's Economic Growth and the ASEAN* (2001).

SHEN Hongfang is professor at the School of Southeast Asian Studies, Xiamen University. She is also a senior fellow at the Institute of Southeast Asian Studies and a concurrent professor at the Finance Department of the College of Economics. She received her PhD in Economics from Beijing University. Her research focuses on East Asian trade and economic relations, and Southeast Asian economies, in particular, Philippines and Thailand.

ASEAN and China: Towards A Harmonious Relationship

Lai Hongyi and Lim Tin Seng

The Association of Southeast Asian Nations (ASEAN) relations with China have undergone profound changes since official contacts began more than 15 years ago. In July 1991 and at the invitation of Malaysia, Chinese Foreign Minister Qian Qichen, who represented China as a Consultative Partner of ASEAN, attended the 24th ASEAN Ministerial Meeting (AMM) in Kuala Lumpur. Multilateral dialogues to promote cooperation, regional peace and economic development between ASEAN and China have significantly improved their relations. In fact, the deepening China-ASEAN relations have aroused strong interests from the media, policymakers and experts worldwide.

In retrospect, China-Southeast Asia relations went through fairly rough times. During the Cold War China's relations with the original ASEAN members, namely, Indonesia, Malaysia, Singapore, Thailand and Philippines, were one of animosity. From the mid 1960s to mid 1970s, Beijing placed ideological alignment over state-to-state relations by supporting Communist insurgents in non-communist countries and implicitly granting ethnic Chinese in the region citizen status when they travelled to China. These moves aroused suspicion from the aforesaid Southeast Asian nations and strained its relations with ASEAN. In fact, in order to contain any expansion of communist influence in the region these Southeast Asian countries had formed organisations such as the ASEAN in 1967 and participated in numerous security or political forums with external powers such as the United States and Japan, most notably the Southeast Asian Treaty Organisation in 1954.

However, from the 1970s to the early 1990s, relationship between the two sides took a positive turn. This was facilitated by Mao Zedong's decision to realign China's foreign policy towards the United States in the early 1970s and Deng Xiaoping's announcement to stop China's support of communist parties in the region and to regard ethnic Chinese from Southeast Asia as foreigners in the late 1970s. These acts, especially those by Deng, removed major irritants in China's relations with ASEAN and eased fears among ASEAN members. In the 1980s China's economic reform and open-door policy suggested to ASEAN that China was committed to economic development and economic reform, instead of a communist revolution. Both sides also found trade and investment a broad and new area for cooperation.

Since 1989 and especially 1992, ASEAN-China relations have taken place against a backdrop of an international debate on China's domestic politics, China's rise and the best approach to dealing with China. It has been accepted by many analysts in international relations that a rising power tends to upset the existing balance of power and induce regional and even global tension and conflict. For a few years, especially after the 1989 Tiananmen incident, many in the West perceived China as the last stronghold of the outdated communism, as well as an international security threat. They advocated a policy of keeping China at arm's length and containing it if possible.[1]

After the 1989 Tiananmen incident, instead of sanctioning China, key players in the ASEAN, including Indonesia and Singapore, established diplomatic ties with Beijing in 1990 while Brunei did so in 1991. By 1991, all ASEAN members had established or re-established diplomatic ties with Beijing. China joined the ASEAN Regional Forum in 1994. Remarkably, the positive momentum was not derailed by the heated territorial disputes over the Spratly Islands in the South China Sea between China and Vietnam from 1992–1994 and between China

---

[1]For a portrait of China's inevitable conflict with the United States, refer to R. Bernstein and R. H. Munro, *The Coming Conflict with China*. New York: A.A. Knopf, 1997. For a more balanced analysis, refer to Samuel Kim, ed. *China and the World: Chinese Foreign Relations in the Post-Cold War Era*. Boulder, CO: Westview Press, 1994; Yong Deng and Fei-ling Wang, eds. *China Rising: Power and Motivation in Chinese Foreign Policy*. Lanham: Rowman & Littlefield Publishers, 2005.

and the Philippines in 1995.[2] At the 29th AMM in Jakarta in 1996, ASEAN upgraded China from a Consultative Partner, which it had been since 1991, to full Dialogue Partner status. As ASEAN expanded its membership to include Vietnam in 1995, Laos and Myanmar in 1997 and Cambodia in 1999, China worked with the grouping to improve the status of ASEAN. In 1997, leaders from ASEAN countries and China held the first informal summit in Kuala Lumpur, Malaysia, to officially recognise the ASEAN-China process and to adopt the strategy of "good neighbourliness" and "mutual trust" to strengthen and expand existing ASEAN-China ties in the 21st century.

ASEAN-China relations improved even further after 1997. Beijing's decision not to devalue the Reminbi during the Asian financial crisis amid international pressure and the multi-billion-dollar financial assistance to Southeast Asian and Asian nations won the admiration of ASEAN countries. The signing of the Declaration on the Conduct of Parties in the South China Sea in 2002 between China and ASEAN worked to further ease territorial disputes and paved the way for joint exploration in the area. More importantly, deepening economic interdependency in the region helped elevate ASEAN-China partnership to a new level of cooperation and integration. This cumulated in the landmark conclusion of the China-ASEAN Comprehensive Economic Cooperation Agreement in 2002, which provides for the establishment of an ASEAN-China Free Trade Area.[3]

In sum, ASEAN-China relations have evolved from one that was plagued with suspicion and scepticism to one that characterises a dynamic and friendly partnership. In a sense, this testifies to the success of China's peaceful, flexible and adroit diplomacy in the reform era. Indeed, China's success in Southeast Asia has earned high marks from analysts. Leading China scholars in the United States observed with envy and admiration. One wrote:

---

[2]For a historical overview and analysis of China's relations with Southeast Asia, refer to Lai Hongyi's chapter in this book.

[3]For an earlier discussion on China-ASEAN relations, refer to Saw Swee-Hock, Sheng Lijun, and Chin Kin Wah, eds. *ASEAN-China Relations: Realities and Prospects*. Singapore: Institute of Southeast Asian Studies, 2005. This volume was based on a conference held in June 2004.

China generally has done a very effective job in recent years in changing the perspective of Southeast Asian nations toward viewing China's emergence as a net benefit rather than a threat, particularly on the economic front... US impatience with regional "talk shops" and the "ASEAN way" has provided China with a strategic opportunity to enhance its position in Southeast Asia, of which Beijing has clearly taken full advantage.[4]

Nevertheless, what these analysts have missed is that ASEAN also appreciates China's inputs in the consolidation and development of ASEAN and regional integration. As Professor Tommy Koh notes in the "Roundtable Discussion" in this book, China's interest in ASEAN and economic integration with the region kick started a healthy competitive process. Major players in the region, including Japan, South Korea, India, Australia, New Zealand and the United States, were also pressured to court ASEAN. This drives economic and political integration in the region and enhances the status of ASEAN, providing ample reasons for ASEAN to renew and strengthen itself.

To mark the 15th anniversary of ASEAN-China relations, the East Asian Institute of the National University of Singapore organised a symposium in December 2006. This book is based on the papers presented at the symposium. Unique to this volume is that both practitioners and scholars offer their analyses of the current state of ASEAN-China relations as well as their suggestions for improvements. In one of the speeches, the ASEAN Secretary-General and Minister of State for Education and Manpower reflects on the achievements of the relations and offers valuable suggestions to meeting remaining challenges in the relations. Authors of individual chapters include leading scholars and established analysts from China, Indonesia, Malaysia, Singapore, the Philippines, Vietnam, Myanmar and Laos. They came from leading think tanks and prominent universities in these countries. As some of them are directly involved in the policy deliberation in their home countries, their views are thus representative of their colleagues back home.

---

[4]C. Fred Bergsten, Bates Gill, Nicholas R. Lardy, and Derek Mitchell, *China: The Balance Sheet*. New York: Public Affairs, 2006, pp. 133–134.

The papers in this volume cover the strategic and political framework of the relations, as well as economic issues such as trade and investment. They are categorised into papers and discussion papers according to their length and theme. The papers offer well-grounded analyses of issues that have caught considerable attention, such as China-Myanmar relations, sustainability of China's economic rise and its regional implication, and China-Singapore economic relations. Some papers also offer valuable insights into relatively unexplored issues, such as limits in China's economic leverage in the region, lingering concerns about China's rise, and China-Vietnam relations. Putting them together, these papers constitute a balanced, diverse and up-to-date diagnosis of the development and state of China-ASEAN relations as well as economic integration of East and Southeast Asia. The following section outlines their arguments and findings.

Putting Changing China-ASEAN Relations into Perspective

Part I of the book contains opening speeches from senior officials from ASEAN and Singapore. In his speech, Minister of State for Education and Manpower Gan Kim Yong comments on the evolving ASEAN-China relations within the political, economical and socio-cultural framework for the past 15 years. The signing of agreements, such as the China-ASEAN Comprehensive Economic Cooperation Agreement in 2002 and the Treaty of Amity and Cooperation in 2003, has significantly strengthened and deepened the bilateral relationship. He also notes that recent developments such as the signing of the two ASEAN-China economic cooperation documents in Cebu, as well as the progress made in the services and investment chapters of the ASEAN-China FTA, have prompted other regional countries to promote their bilateral relations with ASEAN.

Ong Keng Yong, the ASEAN Secretary-General, also reflects on the gradual improvement of ASEAN-China relations since 1991. He suggests that the improvement in ties is attributed to joint efforts in finding innovative and mutually beneficial ways to deal with challenges and move the relationship forward. Relations are thus complementary in every field, facilitating the integration of ASEAN and China.

Nevertheless, ASEAN and China should continue to build upon their achievements to meet future challenges. One of the ways is for China to support ASEAN's initiatives such as the East Asia Summit and to help narrowing the development gap among ASEAN member countries.

Despite impressive improvement in ASEAN-China relations, there remains, as Jusuf Wanandi points out, certain scepticism in some ASEAN countries on the motives and intention of China. He highlights a few areas where China can help to reduce the uneasiness of ASEAN members and maintain a high-level cooperation to promote mutual trust and understanding. For example, as far as territorial disputes in the South China Sea are concerned, Beijing can conclude the Code of Conduct in the South China Sea and explain its claim in the area. Moreover, China can participate actively in ASEAN's initiatives such as the development of the Greater Mekong Sub-region and help out the underdeveloped ASEAN members. Furthermore, China should also introduce more socio-cultural initiatives to foster stronger people-to-people ties.

Political and Security Dimensions

Politics and security have always been one of the top priority areas of cooperation between ASEAN and China since 1991. Part II of the book is devoted to this topic. Southeast Asia and China have come a long way in uplifting their relations to the current high level. Lai Hongyi tracks and explains the evolution of China's relations with Southeast Asia from the mid 1960s to the present. He suggests that the ups and downs in China's relations with Southeast Asian nations can be explained by China's domestic development, relations between major powers (including China, the United States and the Soviet Union), ideology, and political and economic geography. He argues that China's peaceful rise is integral to China's smooth economic reform and development and that in the years to come China and Southeast Asia can be expected to deepen their ties and cooperation while managing contentious issues.

Sheng Lijun's paper, however, offers an alternative perspective to the rapidly improving and expanding China-ASEAN relations. It states that even though relations between the two sides have improved considerably, most ASEAN nations, especially the original ASEAN members — Indonesia, Malaysia, Philippines, Singapore and Thailand — still maintain strong relations with the West. This shows that core ASEAN countries still have reservation over a rising China and do not want China to disrupt the existing balance of power in the region. Moreover, the impact of ASEAN's growing economic cooperation with China is still small compared to that with the West and Japan.

To fully understand political and security ties between China and ASEAN, it is necessary to look at China's relationship with certain ASEAN countries. Li Chenyang's paper studies the controversial relationship between China and Myanmar. It highlights the traditional paukphaw (brotherhood) which the two countries enjoy even after the formation of the Myanmar military regime in September 1988. China and Myanmar have constructed a mutually beneficial partnership in political, economic and security aspects. Both sides are presently trying to expand socio-cultural exchanges. However, Myanmar has been assertive politically in its effort to balance its relations with China and those with ASEAN, India and other powers, and to withstand foreign intervention in its domestic politics. The paper concludes that it is incorrect to say that Myanmar is a pawn of China and to regard China as having stymied democratisation in Myanmar.

It would be interesting to study the bilateral relations between two fastest growing economies, Vietnam in ASEAN and China in the world. Do Tien Sam describes and analyses the achievements and issues in Vietnam China relations since the normalisation of bilateral relations in 1991, especially in the demarcation of the land border and the Tonkin Gulf. Vietnam-China economic cooperation in trade, investment and tourism has been substantial. Both sides have also expanded socio-cultural exchanges. Although a number of outstanding problems have yet to be solved, particularly the demarcation issue in the South China Sea and trade deficits, Vietnam-China relations are likely to improve especially when the ASEAN-China Free Trade Area is taking gradual effect.

Ignatius Wibowo Wibisono, however, paints a bleaker picture of the political and security implications of China in ASEAN. By gathering the views from government officials and academics in Indonesia, the paper presents a converging perception that China can pose a danger either now or in the future for Indonesia and the region. Although it pointed out that there is a warming of ties between Indonesia and China in recent years, Indonesia remains very cautious about a rising China. For China to cross this barrier, it has to promote more socio-cultural exchanges with Indonesia and the region to strengthen its soft power.

In her paper, Wang Yan cautions against exaggerating the effects of China's rise because other developing nations such as Brazil, India and Russia are also rising and also because China has remained relatively under-developed. She discusses how the Chinese government adopted measures to minimise concerns over China's rise in the region. These measures include promoting and participating in multilateral regional schemes like the signing of the Treaty of Amity and Cooperation and the Joint Declaration on Strategic Partnership for Peace and Prosperity, and supporting the ASEAN vision of regional integration.

Despite differing opinions towards the effects of China's rise on ASEAN-China relations, it is a fact that China's economic rise has helped propel a higher level of regional cooperation and integration. As pointed out in Zhang Zhenjiang's paper, the rapid expansion and improvement of ASEAN-China bilateral relations has become the new engine for East Asian regionalism. Japan and South Korea were once reluctant to institutionalise regionalism with ASEAN even though both are dialogue partners and enjoy strong economic relations with ASEAN. They are now initiating the same level of cooperation as that of China with ASEAN.

The optimism in China's relations with ASEAN countries is also reflected in Bounnheuang Songnavong's paper. Though China-Laos bilateral trade is among the smallest in ASEAN, China has launched a number of initiatives with Laos. In particular, it is providing financial assistance to Laos in terms of regional funds, such as programmes for the development of the Mekong Basin, the ASEAN Economic Fund and ASEAN Development Fund. These initiatives have encouraged the Laotian government to expand its cooperation with China in trade, investment and tourism.

Aung Kyaw Oo, director of a leading think tank in international affairs in Myanmar, provides a Myanmar's perspective to China's relationship with Myanmar. He traces the ups and downs in Myanmar-China relations since 1949. He suggests that the close relationship between the two countries is largely attributed to their increasing economic interdependency and Beijing's consistency in upholding the five principles of peaceful co-existence and its peaceful development foreign policy.

Economic Relations

After ASEAN and China established official contact in 1991, economic cooperation between the two sides expanded rapidly. Part III of the book focuses on the economic implications of their relations. From 1991 to 2000, ASEAN-China bilateral trade grew at about 17 percent a year and the trade volume expanded from US$7.9 billion to US$39.5 billion. After China joined the WTO in 2001, total trade volume increased at an even faster pace of more than 20 percent per annum during the 2001–2006 period. Trade volume grew to US$145.2 billion in 2006. It is anticipated to hit US$200 billion by 2010. Furthermore, from 2001 to 2006, ASEAN as a whole enjoyed hefty trade surplus in their trade with China. The rapid growth in ASEAN-China trade is largely due to the continuing development of ASEAN countries, the strong economic performance of the Chinese economy and regional economic initiatives such as the ASEAN-China Free Trade Area. Lu Jianren examines the reasons and regional effects of China's high growth. Besides a trade surplus, ASEAN countries reap a number of benefits from China's economic growth—the ASEAN-China Free Trade Area, investment from China's enterprises, China's growing assistance with capacity building, China's increasing foreign aid, financial stability due to a strong and even stronger Renminbi maintained by China, and deepening economic integration powered by China's economic growth. As a result, it is likely that China and ASEAN will continue to forge a closer economic partnership.

The aforementioned macro view on China-ASEAN economic cooperation is buttressed by studies of economic ties between China and individual ASEAN countries. Zhao Hong's discussion on Singapore's economic relations with China focuses on Singapore's investment in China. In 2005, Singapore invested about US$28 billion in China, more than a quarter of its total investment in Asia. Zhao indicates that Singapore companies are now shifting their investment from labour-intensive to high-tech industries. In addition, Singapore companies are also acquiring or in joint ventures with Chinese companies. Some Singapore investors are also helping to develop the central and western regions of China by developing the regions' agricultural sector and the northeast through setting up a "Singapore City". Zhao highlights areas where Singapore can expand its investment in China and attract China's investment.

Teng Siow Song studies Singapore's economic relationship with China. He first discusses East Asia's trade with China and regional impact of China's rise. He emphasises that China has become a catalyst of regional economic integration. Branding Singapore-China relations as "unique", he discusses how Singapore's perception of China evolved over the years, especially after establishing diplomatic ties with China in 1991. As China's largest trading partner and largest investor in Southeast Asia in 2006, Singapore has endorsed many bilateral economic agreements with China and is very supportive of China's initiatives to promote greater regional integration in ASEAN.

Scholars take up macro economic themes in the discussion papers. Liao Shaolian, for example, discusses the implications of China's economic growth in ASEAN. One implication is the growing trade and economic interdependence between ASEAN and China. The other is increasing investment and tourists. By the end of 2005, China's total foreign direct investment (FDI) in ASEAN accumulated to only US$1.2 billion. This is only a fraction of ASEAN's total FDI in China, which is about US$38.5 billion. However, China's recent move to decentralise approval of investment abroad, as well as regional agreements such as the Agreement on Avoidance of Double Taxation, will result in an increase in China's FDI to ASEAN in the future.

Other scholars provide close-up analyses of economic relations be-tween China and other ASEAN countries. Singapore's closest neighbour, Malaysia, is also enjoying good relations with China. Stephen Leong gives a concise but informative review of Malaysia's relations with China in the last half century. He discusses how Malaysia has capitalised on Beijing's diplomatic initiatives to further bilateral ties and benefitted from China's spectacular economic growth. Malaysia is currently China's second largest trading partner in ASEAN after Singapore. In 2006, total bilateral trade volume was about US$36 billion. In 2005, Malaysia's investment in China totalled US$247.03 million and Chinese investment in Malaysia was US$19.7 million. Malaysia has also been targeting China as a huge tourism market. Chinese tourist arrivals were expected to increase by 20 percent from 2005 to reach 420,000 in 2006.

The Philippines, as Ellen Palanca states, has also reached a "golden age of partnership" with China. The Philippines no longer harps on the "China threat" theory. It has been enjoying growing surplus in its trade with China. Both sides are now expanding ties in various fields ranging from security and defence to people-to-people exchanges. Concomitant with the deepening ties, as Sheng Hongfang reveals in her paper, is a sea change in Philippines' perception of China. She also explains partly how the "golden age of partnership" was constructed. The Philippines viewed China as a threat even years after both sides established diplomatic relations in 1975. This is largely due to the territorial disputes in the South China Sea and the large trade deficit that Philippines registered in its trade with China. However, after the establishment of the ASEAN-China dialogue in 1991, Beijing and Manila worked together through bilateral and multilateral channels to resolve their differences. With dialogues and cooperation in these and many areas between the two nations, the Philippines starts to dismiss the China threat argument and embraces a more positive view of China.

Building Harmonious Relations

For the past 16 years, ASEAN and China have ironed out many differences through its unique multilateral establishment. Through signing the Treaty of Amity and Cooperation, forming an ASEAN-China Free Trade Area and maintaining its "peaceful development" foreign policy in the region, China suggests that as the world's fastest growing economy it is willing to promote stronger ties with ASEAN.

Although some ASEAN countries especially those who had a troubled history with China still harp on the "China threat" theory and remains sceptical about the intention and motives of a rising China, the greater economic interdependency will continue to ease such fears in the future.

The sustainability of this partnership is dependent on whether both sides are willing to continue and uphold the present level of cooperation. During the China-ASEAN Commemorative Summit held at Nanning in October 2006, ASEAN and Chinese leaders agreed to enhance the strategic partnership between the two sides. Noting the growing economic ties, the leaders pledged in their joint statement that they will not only continue to cement and strengthen existing political and security ties, but also expand socio-cultural cooperation. Most notably, the leaders reaffirmed their long-term commitment to establishing an East Asia community through the utilisation of various regional institutions such as the ASEAN Regional Forum, ASEAN Plus Three and East Asia Summit. At the 10th China-ASEAN Summit in Cebu of the Philippines in January 2007, ASEAN and China signed an agreement on Trade in Services of the China-ASEAN Free Trade Area. The agreement will come into force in July 2007. The accord will liberalise sectors ranging from tourism, financial services and telecoms to energy and computers. It also grants services suppliers easier market access and national treatment in specified sectors or sub-sectors. The agreement aims to expand trade in services in the region. Intensified economic ties will generate sustainable development and prosperity and usher in peace in the region. In the years ahead it is reasonable to expect China-ASEAN relations to grow and mature and the region to enter a new age of integration, peace, prosperity and good neighbourliness.

Part I

China-ASEAN Relations: A Key to the Region's Stability and Prosperity

Gan Kim Yong[*]

Since the establishment of the ASEAN-China dialogue, China-ASEAN relation has broadened and deepened considerably, making it one of the most dynamic amongst ASEAN Dialogues. A Commemorative Summit to mark the 15th anniversary of China-ASEAN relation was held in Nanning end October 2006 to celebrate this milestone. A Joint Statement outlining future cooperation was also released at the event as a signal of continued commitment on the part of ASEAN and China in the development of this relationship.

The ASEAN-China relationship has been a mutually beneficial one. The emergence of China has sent shock waves throughout the world and posed a great challenge to the less competitive economies. However, with time, China proves that it is an important engine of growth for the region, and ASEAN countries have benefitted from China's rapid economic growth over the past two decades. The ASEAN-China FTA, with its goods chapter already in force, is a key driver of regional integration. China is now one of the top trading partners for Singapore as well as Thailand, Malaysia and Vietnam. ASEAN is among the top five trading partners for China. Bilateral trade has grown almost eight times from US$17 billion in 1996 to US$130 billion in 2005. China's investments in ASEAN have also been increasing steadily, reaching

[*]Mr. Gan Kim Yong is the Minister of State for Education and Manpower. This paper is adapted from Mr. Gan's opening address at the "ASEAN-China Relations: Harmony and Development" symposium on 18 December 2006.

US$158 million in 2005. There is also cooperation between China and ASEAN countries in various sub-regional initiatives such as the Great Mekong Sub-region Development Zone and Brunei Darussalam-Indonesia-Malaysia-The Philippines-East ASEAN Growth Area (BIMP-EAGA).

The signing of the two ASEAN-China cooperation documents (Second Protocol to amend the Framework Agreement on Comprehensive Economic Cooperation between ASEAN and China, and Protocol to amend the Agreement on Trade in Goods of the ASEAN-China FTA) in Cebu was most encouraging, as it paved the way for the smooth implementation of the ASEAN-China FTA. They include determining and revising the lists of specially designated early-harvest products between China and some ASEAN countries. Work on the services chapter of the ASEAN-China FTA has largely been completed while the investments chapter should similarly be concluded early. The ASEAN-China FTA has also prompted many other dialogue partners to work on FTAs with ASEAN or on other initiatives that are mutually beneficial. For example, an ASEAN-China Fully Liberalised Air Services Agreement will greatly enhance connectivity between ASEAN and China and thereby facilitate people-to-people interaction and boost trade and investment.

In terms of political and security cooperation, ASEAN and China are also working on confidence building measures. One key development is the signing of the Declaration on the Conduct of Parties in the South China Sea in 2002 as a gesture of good neighbourliness on the part of China. Overall, China has played a constructive role in establishing a strategic partnership for peace and prosperity with ASEAN; the signing of the Treaty of Amity and Cooperation in 2003, the first between ASEAN and a Dialogue Partner, is a significant milestone for China-ASEAN relations. In addition, China has strongly supported the ASEAN Regional Forum and Southeast Asia Nuclear Weapon Free Zone. All these have encouraged other regional countries to also look at stepping up their relations with ASEAN.

Singapore views ASEAN's relationship with China as one of the key dynamics contributing to regional stability and prosperity. Since China's reform and opening up in the late 1970s, Singapore has been a strong proponent of the importance of China to the region as well as the constructive role China can play. Singapore has encouraged ASEAN and China to continue engaging in dialogue and working together through various regional channels including ASEAN+3, APEC, ASEM, ARF and the EAS. As China-ASEAN relations enter the next phase of development, the continued strengthening of ASEAN's relations with China remains a win-win outcome for all, contributing to a peaceful, prosperous and vibrant Asia. The rise of China has no doubt posed new political, security and economic challenges to the region. Therefore, it is important for both academics and scholars to continue to engage in issues that may impact China-ASEAN ties and to look at ways and means to strengthen the partnership.

Further Enhancing ASEAN-China Relations

Ong Keng Yong

The participation of leaders of ASEAN member countries and China in Nanning at the Commemorative Summit to mark the 15th Anniversary of ASEAN-China Dialogue Relations shows that both ASEAN and China are determined to maintain the close relationship that they had forged. In the coming years it is important that the regular high-level dialogue and consultations among the leaders should continue, as it will help in building mutual trust, confidence and comfort, thus allowing a free flow of frank discussion and exchange of views on issues of common interest. Such atmosphere will certainly serve well for the continuous nurturing of ASEAN-China relations.

Looking back in history, the links between Southeast Asia and China date back to centuries during which individual countries of this region and China carried out trade, cultural interactions and sea voyages.

Collectively, as ASEAN, the relationship between countries in Southeast Asia and China opened up in the year 1991. At the early stage, relations progressed gradually as both sides worked towards achieving a significant level of comfort and confidence. ASEAN and China have always managed to find innovative ways and means to deal with challenges and move the relationship forward.

Sixteen years later one could observe that ASEAN-China relationship has matured. Cooperation has developed in all dimensions, covering various areas of collaboration, in political and security, economics and trade, socio-culture and people-to-people interaction.

Relationship reached a higher level with the signing of the Joint Declaration on Strategic Partnership for Peace and Prosperity in

October 2003 and the adoption of a five-year ASEAN-China Plan of Action to implement the Joint Declaration in November 2004 by the leaders of ASEAN and China. These important documents provide the guide and roadmap for advancing cooperation between the two sides.

Supporting and Complementary Role

ASEAN and China are playing supporting and complementary roles in each other's socio-economic development and in maintaining peace and stability in the region. Many would argue that China is a strong competitor of ASEAN with far reaching impact on the latter's strategic outlook and economic prosperity. On the contrary, ASEAN views the fast growth of China and its development as a positive phenomenon spurring ASEAN to integrate economically and at a faster pace. ASEAN believes that both sides could tap on the complementarities for mutual gains.

ASEAN views China as a close neighbour and an important Dialogue Partner with tremendous potential to offer. With its rapid economic growth and a population of about 1.3 billion people, China is a huge consumer of ASEAN products and also a source of future FDI to the region. In addition, ASEAN is benefitting from the large number of Chinese tourists visiting the region and vice versa. The arrival of tourists from China averaged three million in 2004 and 2005.

China is also supporting ASEAN's integration through the promotion of trade and investment in the region. In addition, it supports various regional integration schemes. China contributed US$1 million to the ASEAN Development Fund and pledged another US$1 million to the implementation of Initiative for ASEAN Integration (IAI) projects. Furthermore, China is involved in the ASEAN Mekong Basin Development Cooperation (AMBDC), the Brunei Indonesia Malaysia Philippines-East ASEAN Growth Area (BIMP-EAGA) and other sub-regional economic initiatives.

ASEAN is now vigorously embarking on its integration and community building efforts to make this region a single market and production base with free-flow of goods, services, investment and skilled labour, and freer flow of capital. All these will further contribute

to the enhancement of ASEAN's economic base, which in turn will also
benefit China.

Enhancing Economic Partnership

Economic cooperation has grown rapidly, especially after the signing of
the Framework Agreement on Comprehensive Economic Cooperation
(CEC), which provides for the establishment of an ASEAN-China Free
Trade Area, scheduled for 2010 for Brunei Darussalam, Indonesia,
Malaysia, the Philippines, Singapore, Thailand and China, and for
Cambodia, Lao PDR, Myanmar and Vietnam to join by 2015.

According to ASEAN's statistics, total trade between ASEAN and
China grew by 27 percent from US$89 billion in 2004 to US$113 billion
in 2005. The contribution of total ASEAN-China trade to total ASEAN
trade with the world also increased from 8.3 percent in 2004 to 9.3
percent in 2005. However, China's foreign direct investment (FDI) to
ASEAN declined by 15 percent from US$670 million in 2004 to US$570
million in 2005. Cumulative (1999–2005) China's FDI to ASEAN
amounted to US$1.4 billion. Certainly, more Chinese companies
can invest substantially in the industrial and job creating sectors of
ASEAN's economies.

The Agreements on Trade in Goods (TIG) and Dispute Settlement
Mechanism under the Framework Agreement on CEC were signed in
November 2004. The Agreement on TIG came into force on 20 July
2005. Business transactions and FDI are expected to increase as a result
of the entering into force of the Agreement on TIG and the reduction
and elimination of tariffs. The Agreement on Trade in Services between
ASEAN and China is expected to be signed soon. Negotiations on the
agreement on investment are ongoing.

One area for both sides to work on is infrastructure development
to accelerate ASEAN's economic growth. China's investment here will
also narrow the development gaps among ASEAN member countries. A
good systematic approach will be beneficial to China's inner provinces
such as Yunnan, Sichuan, etc.

Promoting People-To-People Exchange

On socio-cultural cooperation, there have been several activities organised by ASEAN and China to enhance people-to-people exchanges and promote public awareness among the peoples of ASEAN and China. While the business sector has established several events such as the annual ASEAN-China Expo and ASEAN-China Business and Investment Summit to help match-making, networking and expanding business linkages, more is needed to be done to ensure other sections of the population — government officials, youths, civil society and intellectuals — could interact to comprehensively strengthen ASEAN-China dialogue.

Basically, information on ASEAN and China must be more effectively disseminated to all segments of the society. More websites, greater news coverage and documentaries should be made available to reach out to a large spectrum of audiences, both in ASEAN and China. China's announcement at the ASEAN-China Commemorative Summit in October 2006 in Nanning that it would invite 1,000 youths from ASEAN member countries to visit China and to train 8,000 ASEAN professionals in different fields in the coming five years are good gestures in fostering people-to-people interaction, especially among the young people.

Moving into the Future

The ASEAN-China dialogue has developed steadily over the past 15 years. The broad-based cooperation is guided by well-thought out plans and a long-term vision. To a large extent, strong political will on both sides ensure that the relations are properly nurtured and strengthened in a calibrated manner.

However, ASEAN and China should not take their past accomplishments for granted since the region and the world are constantly changing. As such the relationship would face various new opportunities and challenges, and the way forward would be for ASEAN and China to continue to build upon their achievements. It is also vital for both sides to manage potential challenges with utmost care by taking into account the overall state of the relationship and the bigger strategic picture.

In the coming years, ASEAN and China will continue to strengthen their cooperation and implement what both sides have committed to do, especially the realisation of the FTA so that it would bring about more tangible benefits to the peoples of ASEAN and China. Moreover, both sides will have to work closely to address challenges facing the region such as transnational crime and terrorism, SARS, avian influenza and natural disasters.

With rapid development in the region, ASEAN has initiated new projects such as the East Asia Summit (EAS) and the FTA strategy to manage regional affairs and challenges. China's support for ASEAN's initiatives is essential for their success. A cohesive and strong ASEAN is in China's own interest. Narrowing the developmental gaps among ASEAN member countries is a key strategy for building a cohesive and strong ASEAN. China can play a big role in this ASEAN endeavour.

Looking into the immediate future, another idea worth deliberating is how ASEAN and China should pursue the envisioned East Asia community. This visionary concept is firing the imagination of many scholars and thinkers. The question is how to convert the existing multi-faceted and multi-layered relationships around the region into a community-based relationship without causing undue stress and tension. The ASEAN Plus Three framework and mechanisms have been developed over the past ten years. They must be built upon to obtain a greater value-add while the vast potential of the EAS is being tapped.

Overcoming Obstacles in ASEAN-China Relations

Jusuf Wanandi

There have been many changes in ASEAN-China relations in the last 16 years, especially after China became a dialogue partner of ASEAN and an active member of the ASEAN Regional Forum and the ASEAN Plus Three Process, signed the Treaty of Amity and Cooperation (TAC) and proposed a Free Trade Agreement (FTA) with ASEAN. However, the history of ASEAN-China relationship was full of prejudices and even indirect conflicts caused by China's Communist Party subversion and infiltration of Southeast Asia. These were terminated following Deng Xiaoping's visit to a number of Southeast Asian countries in 1979, which began a new era of ASEAN-China relations. This was followed by the normalisation of relations between China and the last of ASEAN members, namely Indonesia, Singapore and Brunei in 1990 and 1991.

Because of China's history, size, as well as spectacular economic growth of 9 to 10 percent per annum in the last 25 years or so, there is lingering "un-easiness" with China in Southeast Asia, a natural response for smaller countries living next to a "huge" country with a history of negativities. China has to take this fact into account and try to accommodate some of the worries of ASEAN members.

In particular, China can do two things to address uneasiness amongst ASEAN members. One is to conclude the Code of Conduct on the South China Sea whose principles have been agreed upon several years ago. The conclusion of the Code could provide assurances to ASEAN members, especially those who have a claim on some atolls and islands in the South China Sea. The other is to explain what exactly

China's claim in the South China Sea consists of, because China still has, in its map, the nine points of dotted lines some of which are near the border with the Natuna island, which overlaps with Indonesia's exclusive economic zone (EEZ).

China has promised to assist ASEAN in overcoming the economic divide between new and old members. One effective way is for China to cooperate closely with ASEAN members on the development of the Greater Mekong Sub-region (GMS), a critical project for most new ASEAN members who are still under-developed and dependent on the water level of the river. Their lifeline depends on China's willingness to maintain the water flow from the upper level of the river in Yunnan province. The water flow could easily be affected by the size and number of dams (which is about 12) that China will be constructing in the future. As a member of the GMS development schemes, China should take the development plan of rivers in Yunnan into consideration.

The economic opening of China to ASEAN, as has been formulated in the ASEAN-China Comprehensive Economic Cooperation proposed by then Premier Zhu Rongji, has been a very astute and generous gesture which has helped alleviate earlier worries due to China's rise and competition. With further efforts in the area of investment, including from China into ASEAN, cooperation on energy security and environment, infrastructure developments, and pandemic issues such as SARS and Avian-flu, China-ASEAN relations have leapfrogged to one that is mutually beneficial. It has also brought forth attention from both sides to the issue of human security at the same time. These efforts show how important the relationship has become in 15 years with economics underpinning the relationship.

ASEAN members of the ASEAN-China Eminent Persons Group (EPG) have also made it clear to the Chinese in their meetings that the strategic relationship with China is part of ASEAN's strategic partnership with other great powers in the region, namely US, Japan, Russia and India. It is expected that China also views her strategic partnership with ASEAN on the same basis.

Economics and political relations and cooperation are very important in the equation of ASEAN-China relationship. For the longer term however, the socio-cultural aspects and people-to-people relations are equally important. That is why relations in education, art and culture, sports and youth, are so important for mutual understanding and trust, which in East Asia context, is particularly critical for regional community building.

Part II

Political and Security Dimensions

China's Evolving Relations with Southeast Asia: Domestic and Strategic Factors

Lai Hongyi

The rise of China is one of the most important events in the new century and is likely to profoundly shape future world events. As China's neighbours, Southeast Asia feels immediately the effects of China's external conduct. China's peaceful course of ascendance since the late 1970s has been, by and large, positive development for most of Southeast Asia. This article seeks to track and explain the evolution of China's strategy for peaceful rise and examine China's relations with Southeast Asia from the 1960s to the present. It also suggests that a host of factors accounted for the ups and downs of China's foreign relations in the past four decades. These include China's domestic development, relations between big powers, political and economic geography, and political ideology. While these factors combined to render China's relations with most of Southeast Asia fragile and even hostile in the 1960s, they have also led to the deepening of relations since the mid 1990s.

The most noticeable factor shaping China's foreign relations is China's domestic development. Mao's provocative diplomacy and domestic radicalism had damaged China's ties with Southeast Asia from 1965 to 1970, and to a lesser extent from 1971 to 1978. It was China's shift away from Mao's radicalism to economic reform and development since the late 1970s that has paved the way for China's reconciliation with Southeast Asia. Since 1979, China's diplomacy has taken a more peaceful path, accumulating to the pronouncement of a strategy of China's peaceful rise in 2003. The notion of peaceful rise has been widely associated with foreign policy under President Hu

Jintao.[1] Nevertheless, as Avery Goldstein argued in his book on China's international strategy and as Zheng Bijian, the Chinese proponent of peaceful rise reminded us, peaceful rise is an extension of Deng's concept of "peace and development".[2]

Relations with big powers have cast a long shadow over China's relations with Southeast Asia. In the 1950s China's relations with the US were strained due to the Cold War with many Southeast Asian countries siding the US. They viewed China's support for communism in Asia and especially communist parties in their own countries as hostile moves. Since the improvement in China-US relations in the early 1970s, China's ties with Southeast Asia have also improved.

Furthermore, due to political and economic geography, Southeast Asia would prefer a friendly, benign, well-behaved and prosperous China. Such a China is conducive to regional stability and peaceful relations with Southeast Asia, while contributing to economic growth of the region.

Finally, China and Southeast Asia are free of ideological obstacles, unlike China's relations with the US and the European Union. Both do not view political freedom and liberal democracy as a necessary condition for lasting good relations. Both also do not favour interference in the internal affairs of the other. The difference in ideology explains why China's relations with much of the West were strained in the years after the 1989 Tiananmen incident while its ties with Southeast Asia were relatively unaffected.

The first part of the article gives an overview of China's policies towards Southeast Asia from the 1960s to the present, with special focus on the late 1970s. It argues that China's peaceful strategy towards most of Southeast Asia since the late 1970s initially served its need to align with the United States to counter the Soviet influence. Since the late

---

[1]Zheng Yongnian and Tok Sow Keat, "China's Peaceful Rise (I): Hu-Wen's Core Foreign Policy Strategy," *EAI Background Brief, No. 219*. Singapore: East Asian Institute, National University of Singapore, December 9, 2004, pp. 1, 3–4.

[2]See Avery Goldstein, *Rising to the Challenge: China's Grand Strategy and International Security*. Stanford: Stanford University Press, 2005, p. 192. "Foreword" by John L. Thornton in *China's Peaceful Rise: Speeches of Zheng Bijian, 1997–2005*. Washington, D.C.: Brookings Institution Press, 2005, p. x.

1980s it has become a component in China's good neighbour policies and efforts to forge cooperation and economic integration. The second part of the article makes general observations on China-Southeast Asia relations in the past decades and in the years ahead. It suggests that it is in China's interests to continue its peaceful rise so that political and economic ties with Southeast Asia will continue to deepen.

Evolution of China-Southeast Asia Relations

Rocky Relations, 1965–1970

China's relations with Southeast Asia (especially Indonesia and Indochina) developed and prospered after the Bandung Conference in April 1955. During the 1955–1965 period China's leaders also exchanged visits with those of Burma, Indonesia, Cambodia and Laos. In 1963, State President Liu Shaoqi visited Indonesia, Burma and Laos. China concluded a border treaty and a friendship treaty with Burma in 1960.[3] China's peaceful overtures in this period had to do with its need for economic rebuilding and diplomatic breakthrough after the Korean War.

After 1965, however, China's relations with Southeast Asia deteriorated. Anti-communist movements in Southeast Asia and China's support for communist parties in the region further ruptured bilateral relations. Ethnic Chinese became a cause for disputes between China and Southeast Asia. China broke off relations with Indonesia and refused to recognise the newly independent Malaysia and Singapore.[4]

China's provocation at the world stage was domestically induced. From 1966 to 1970, China was at the peak of its Cultural Revolution. Mao rallied "Red Guards" to attack moderate leaders, who favoured family farming and industrialisation over ideological purity. China even called for worldwide revolution and countered Western encirclement

---

[3]Xie Yixian, *Zhechong yu Gongchu: Xin Zhongguo Duiwai Guangxi 40 Nian (Conflict and Co-Existence: Forty Years of Foreign Policies of New China).* Zhengzhou: Henan Remin Chubanshe, 1990, p. 218.

[4]Lee Kuan Yew, *From Third World to First — The Singapore Story: 1965–2000.* Singapore: Times Editions, 2000, pp. 635–37.

by arming the Vietnamese Communist Party (VCP) to fight the US troops.

Recovery of Ties under late Mao's and Deng's Peaceful Diplomacy (1971–89)

Sensing an imminent Soviet attack and trying to end its diplomatic quandary, China realigned with the US. The US also wanted to withdraw its troops from Vietnam. The Beijing-Washington rapprochement opened up space for Southeast Asia and even Northeast Asia to improve their ties with China and to take a different stance from the US.

China initiated contact with Singapore's diplomats in late 1970.[5] In 1971, in the UN vote on the resolution to accord the seat at the Security Council to the PRC, the Philippines went along with the US opposition stance while Thailand and Indonesia abstained, and Malaysia voted in favour; Singapore also voted in favour in light of the opinion of its majority community.[6] In 1972 Japan established diplomatic ties with China ahead of the US.

China also altered its policy towards overseas Chinese. In 1974 China started to view "overseas Chinese" as citizens of their resident countries and stopped encouraging Chinese overseas to return to China.[7] This paved the way for Chinese rapprochement with Southeast Asian nations. In 1974 and 1975 Malaysia, Philippines and Thailand normalised relations with China while China started to respect Singapore as an independent state in 1974.

In late 1978 Deng became the paramount leader of China. China started to move away from Maoist political and ideological campaigns to economic development. China permitted market forces and pursued economic reform by adopting household farming, setting up special economic zones (SEZs) in Guangdong and Fujian, and opening up to the world economy.

---

[5]Lee, *From Third World to First*, pp. 637–39.
[6]Michael Yahuda, *The International Politics of the Asia-Pacific*. London and New York: RoutledgeCurzon, 2004, p. 84.
[7]Lee, *From Third World to First*, pp. 635–37.

Deng's pragmatic economic agenda produced a sea change in China's foreign policy. Deng maintained that China needed a period of long peace for its domestic development. In this period the US-Soviet-China triangle defined the terms of external peace for China. To ensure its own security China needed to improve ties with its neighbours, cooperate with the US, and contain the influence of the Soviet Union, its arch enemy. As most Southeast Asian nations either were close to the US or maintained formal neutrality, China's ties with them improved quickly. On the other hand, as China acted to check Soviet influence in Indochina, its relations with nations that aligned with the Soviet Union were strained. These nations included Vietnam, Laos and Cambodia.

Meanwhile, in order to promote foreign trade and attract foreign capital for its own economic development as well as to learn from the rapidly growing market economies, China improved ties with maritime Southeast Asia and Thailand.[8] In 1920, on his way to study in France, Deng visited Singapore for two days. In November 1978, Deng visited it again and was impressed by the law and order as well as modernisation of the city. Deng regarded Singapore a model for China. On this trip, Deng also visited Thailand, Malaysia and Burma. China had also improved ties with these nations as well as with the Philippines. Taking advice from then Singapore's Prime Minister Lee Kuan Yew, Deng terminated China's support for communist parties in Southeast Asia. Despite these improvements in China-Southeast Asia ties, well into the 1980s, Indonesia and Malaysia were said to view China as a security concern, though not as serious as before.[9]

In contrast to the improvement in China's relations with maritime Southeast Asia and Thailand, China's relations with Vietnam, Laos and Cambodia deteriorated. As the Vietcong approached its final victory of defeating the United States and unifying the nation, Beijing's indispensable role as a vital ally for Hanoi diminished. China was concerned with Vietnam's ambition to be a leader in Indochina and

---

[8]S.D. Muni, *China's Strategic Engagement with the New ASEAN*. Singapore: Institute of Defence and Strategic Studies, 2002, p. 8.
[9]Ralf Emmers, *Cooperative Security and the Balance of Power in ASEAN and the ARF*. London and New York: RoutledgeCurzon, 2003, p. 133.

to rebuild an Indochina Confederation comprising Vietnam, Laos and Cambodia. Vietnamese troops invaded Cambodia around the turn of 1978 and 1979, initially claiming to retaliate against Khmer Rough's border encroachment and save Cambodians from the regime's genocide. Nevertheless, it effectively controlled the politics and economy of Cambodia. Meanwhile, China was also irritated by Vietnam's bold claims about territories and territorial water, border skirmishes and its expulsion of ethnic Chinese. Hanoi also turned its back on its former patron China, and threw itself into the arms of China's arch rival, the Soviet Union.[10]

In 1979 the Chinese troops launched a brief but relentless war against Vietnam. The Chinese campaign probably earned the acquiescence of the US and some members of the ASEAN who grew weary about Soviet's and Vietnam's expansionism. After the war, ties with the three Indochinese nations were strained; China's relations with these nations started to improve only from 1986, as the Soviet Union under Gorbachev, the VCP after the Sixth Congress and Laos stated their desire to mend ties with Beijing.[11]

Big Improvement in China-Southeast Asia Ties, 1989–1996

The abrupt end to the Tiananmen movement in June 1989 was a watershed in China's relations with the West and with the rest of the world. China's ideological gap with the West and its ideological affinity with the developing world including Southeast Asia came to the limelight and exerted a significant role in the relations. Prior to June 1989, China's relations with the West, especially the United States, had been very warm, and those with the developing world were by and large lukewarm. However, after the Tianamen incident, the situation was reversed. For seven years China's relations with the West precipitated to

---

[10]Liu Hongxuan, *Zhongguo Mulinshi (A History of China's Good Neighbourliness)*. Beijing: Shijie Zhishi Chubanshe, 2001, pp. 378–80; Xie, *Zhechong yu Gongchu: Xin Zhongguo Duiwai Guangxi 40 Nian*, pp. 178–84.

[11]Qian Qichen, *Waijiao Shiji (Ten Stories of Diplomat Qi Qichen)*. Beijing: Shijie Zhishi Chubanshe, 2003, pp. 6–39; Liu Hongxuan, *Zhongguo Mulinshi*, pp. 383, 392.

the bottom and recovered only gradually. Yet China's relations with the Third World including Southeast Asia leapfrogged.

The US, Japan, European Union and G-7 Summit condemned the Tiananmen incident, halted visits of leaders and arms sales to China and postponed new loans from international financial institutions. The period from the late 1980s and the early 1990s was the most difficult time in China's diplomacy in the reform era. China only managed to maintain cordial relations with Japan and Spain.[12] In December 1989, Nicolae Ceaucescu, top leader of Romania, one of the last Communist countries in Europe, was killed in a rebellion. In the eyes of many Western analysts, China was one of the few bastions of communist dictatorial regimes. They started to talk about the China threat. The China threat argument intensified after the collapse of the Soviet Union in December 1991.

Governments in the developing world viewed and treated China differently from the West after the Tianamen incident and the collapse of the Eastern bloc. Many governments in the developing world oppose Western pressure over human rights and see such attempts as flagrant violation of their sovereignty. Singapore, for example, issued a statement deploring the incident, but emphasising the importance of stability and conciliation in China, and avoiding condemning the incident.[13] During the United Nations Assembly after June 1989, leaders and foreign ministers from Asia, Africa and Latin America warmly greeted and met with their Chinese counterparts.[14]

China adopted a dual strategy of managing diplomatic hostilities from the West. On the one hand, it kept a low profile in international affairs while concentrating on developing its economy and solving its domestic problems. As Deng proposed, China should "bide its time and hide its capabilities" at the world stage.

On the other hand, China actively promoted its ties with the developing world, including Southeast Asia. As the Association for Southeast Asian Nations (ASEAN) operates on the principles of non-

---

[12]Qian, *Waijiao Shiji*, pp. 165, 165–98.
[13]Lee, *From Third World to First*, p. 693.
[14]Qian, *Waijiao Shiji*, pp. 198–200.

intervention in internal affairs of member states and decision through consensus, China found Southeast Asia an easier political partner than the West.

In addition, China tapped emerging and rapidly developing markets and their growing foreign capital. In 1990, the five major members of the six-member ASEAN, namely, Indonesia, Malaysia, Philippines, Singapore and Thailand, had a combined population of 316.4 million, gross domestic product (GDP) of $308,320 million, exports of $139,272 million, and imports of $157,944 million. The combined population was equivalent to 27.9 percent that of China while their GDP, exports, and imports were 84.3 percent, 224.3 percent, and 296.1 percent respectively that of China. The five economies also had, on average, a respectable 5 percent per annum growth from 1980–1990, thus constituting a promising economic partner for China, helping it to diversify its trade and reducing its heavy reliance on the western economies.[15]

China's largest breakthrough in its ties with Southeast Asia came when diplomatic ties with Indonesia resumed in 1990. Indonesian President Suharto dropped his demand for an apology from China for its alleged involvement in the failed coup in 1965, for which China denied advance knowledge. On 8 August 1990, China resumed ties with Indonesia, the most populous and influential nation in Southeast Asia. This was followed by Singapore in October 1990 and Brunei in September 1991.[16]

Progress was also made in China's relations with the three Indochina states. Vietnam expressed its support for China's Tiananmen incident. Nguyen Van Linh, the top VCP leader who assumed power in 1986, was a reformist at home and a pragmatist in diplomacy. He favoured the withdrawal of Vietnamese troops from Cambodia and the normalisation of ties with China. In September 1990, Nguyen held a private meeting with the then Chinese President Jiang Zemin and Premier Li Peng in Chengdu, Sichuan. They reached an agreement on the settlement of Cambodia, the most critical obstacle to their bilateral

---

[15]World Bank, *World Development Report 1992*, Washington, D.C.: Oxford University Press, 1992, pp. 218–19, 222–23, 244–45.

[16]Qian, *Waijiao Shiji*, pp. 116–35.

ties. In November 1991, both nations announced the normalisation of relations. By 1996, they had signed nearly 30 cooperation agreements on economy, trade, science and technology, aviation, culture, public security and customs. In October 1991 they signed a treaty to settle border disputes, easing one of the most explosive sources of disputes between them.[17]

Meanwhile, China also kick-started its official contacts with ASEAN. In 1991, China became a Consultative Partner of ASEAN. In the same year, at the invitation of Malaysia, Qian Qichen attended the opening of the 24th ASEAN Ministerial Meeting (AMM) in Kuala Lumpur and expressed China's interest in developing ties with ASEAN. This marked the beginning of China's official contact with ASEAN. In 1994, China and ASEAN established two joint committees for cooperation, one on science and technology, and the other on economy and trade. In 1996, China became a full Dialogue Partner of ASEAN at the 29th AMM in Jakarta.[18]

Nevertheless, two issues cast a shadow over ASEAN's relations with China. One is the disputes over the South China Sea. On the basis of claims of historical administration of the sea, China has been claiming its entire maritime territory. Some analysts regard this claim lacking in legal defence. Vietnam also made historical and occupation claims to the Paracel and Spratly islands; the Philippines made a claim to the largest area of the Spratly called Kalayaan; Malaysia claimed part of the Spratly, and Brunei claimed south of the Spratlys. On his visit to Singapore in August 1990, Chinese Premier Li Peng expressed China's willingness to put aside the territorial dispute and engage in joint exploration and development of the Spratlys with the Southeast Asian nations.

Two developments, however, had made China's promise questionable. In February 1992, China passed the Law on the Territorial Waters and Contiguous Area. It repeated China's claims in the South China Sea and retained the right to use force to protect islands including

---

[17]Qian, *Waijiao Shiji*, pp. 62–3; Liu, Zhongguo Mulinshi, pp. 383–84, 393.
[18]Saw Swee-Hock, Sheng Lijun, and Chin Kin Wah, eds. *ASEAN-China Relations: Realities and Prospects*. Singapore: Institute of Southeast Asian Studies, 2005, pp. 1–2.

the Spratlys and waters around them. In April 1992, China allowed the US-based Creston Energy Corporation to explore oil in the Vanguard Bank, a zone Vietnam claimed as part of its continental shelf. China also promised to protect the corporation militarily if necessary. In 1994, Vietnam granted an oil exploration concession to Mobil Corporation in an area of the Vanguard Bank claimed by China. In February 1995 the Philippines reported of Chinese occupation of Mischief Reef located in the Kalayaan, the first time that China took over territory claimed by an ASEAN member. The Chinese have not repeated similar acts since then.[19]

The other development was China's show of force in the Taiwan Strait in 1995 and 1996. In 1995 Taiwan President Lee Teng Hui gave a highly politicised speech on his visit to his *alma mater*, the Cornell University in the US, for an honorary doctoral degree. The following year he ran for presidential election in Taiwan. In both occasions China conducted missiles tests near Taiwan as a warning to Lee's pro-independence rhetoric. The ASEAN members support one China and view unsympathetically Taiwan's independence. Nevertheless, they are also concerned with the negative political and economic fallouts and the possibility of a war across the Taiwan Strait. They are uncomfortable with rising Chinese nationalism in China's confrontation with Taiwan.

These two developments, especially China's assertive moves in the South China Sea, fanned the China threat perception in Southeast Asia. This, in turn, posed a challenge to the Chinese leadership. They started to realise that much of China's external environment was shaped by the world's perception of China and that China needed to counter the China threat argument through its moderate behaviour and a good explanation about its foreign policy strategy.

New Era of Closer Bonds and Regional Integration: 1997–2002

Since 1997 China-Southeast Asia relations have entered an unprecedented period of friendship and multilateralism. Three developments

---

[19]Ralf Emmers, *Cooperative Security and the Balance of Power in ASEAN and the ARF.* London and New York: RoutledgeCurzon, 2003, pp. 129–35.

paved the way for such a breakthrough in their ties. First, the United States has adopted a strategy of engaging China, despite a brief interlude of hostilities. Despite his China-bashing presidential campaign rhetoric, President Clinton decided to de-link China's most favourite nation trading status from its human rights record. After the PLA missile tests in the Taiwan Strait in 1995–1996 both China and the US realised that confrontation could escalate into a large scale war and unnecessarily inflict heavy casualties and losses on both sides. Both nations have since worked hard to repair their ties. After 1997 US President Clinton pursued a strategy of engaging China. President Jiang visited the US in 1997 and Clinton returned a visit in 1998. Both pledged to build "constructive strategic partnership". Clinton pledged the "Three Nos", promising to restrain Taiwan independence.[20] However, Sino-American ties suffered temporary setbacks following the NATO bombing of the Chinese embassy in Belgrade in May 1999, George W. Bush's "China as a strategic competitor" rhetoric in the 2000 presidential campaign and the US-China plane collision in April 2001. However, leaders of both sides were quick at damage control and resurrected ties. President Bush also wanted to develop constructive working relations with China, especially after the 9/11 terror attacks of the US in 2001. Decent Sino-American relations again offer breathing space for Southeast Asia to further its relations and interaction with China.

Second, the Asian financial crisis in 1997 was a wake-up call to Asian economic unity and the drive towards regional integration. For many Asian nations, the crisis demonstrated risks in permitting hot money from the West to flow in and out of the border without good institutional safeguards against its erosive effects. The West's largely aloof response to the crisis as well as the international financial institutions' rigid requirements in offering rescues also prompted Southeast Asian nations to develop their collective strength in managing crises.

Through helping Southeast Asia countries to weather the crisis, China earned trust from its neighbours. In 1998, in the wake of the

---

[20]See David Lampton, *Same Bed, Different Dreams — Managing US-China Relations, 1989–2000*. Berkely: University of California Press, 2001, pp. 33–63.

crisis, China not only did not devalue its currency, but also generously offer economic aid without prior conditions. In addition, China offered aid of $4 billion to Southeast Asia through the International Monetary Fund (IMF) and bilateral channels. It also provided Indonesia export credits and free emergency medicine.[21] The Chinese supportive moves were in sharp contrast to Tokyo's yen devaluation and the US-led IMF's demanding prerequisites for lending to troubled Southeast Asian nations.

Third, China has made greater strides towards integrating with the world economy and embracing cooperation and multilateralism in world politics. It has also polished its diplomatic skills and developed a clearer strategy to guide its ascendance. Prior to 1996 China viewed regional organisation with plenty of reservation and purposefully refrained from joining any multilateral regional organisations. It participated only in very loosely-structured regional forums such as the APEC, or in a very non-committing manner, such as becoming a Consultative Partner of ASEAN in 1991.

In 1996, China started to embrace multilateralism by signing military confidence building pacts with Russia, Kazakhstan, Kyrgyzstan and Tajikistan in 1996, which paved the way for the Shanghai Cooperation Organisation.[22] In late 1999, China concluded a landmark agreement with the US over its accession to the World Trade Organisation (WTO). China joined the WTO in late 2001. This move signalled China's unprecedented will to be a stakeholder in the existing regime of the world economy. The catch phrase "a responsible big power" has been surfacing in official media and speeches since 1999.[23] China realised that by integrating with multilateral institutions it could establish a favourable image and even forge mutually beneficial relationships with major powers and the region.

---

[21]Policy Research Office, Ministry of Foreign Affairs of the PRC, eds. *Zhongguo Waijiao (China's Diplomacy)*. Beijing: Shijie Zhishi Chubanshe, 1999, p. 19.

[22]Goldstein, *Rising to the Challenge*, pp. 118–22.

[23]For evidence of the use of the phrase, refer to the series of official annals on China's foreign affairs: Policy Research Office, Ministry of Foreign Affairs of the PRC, eds. *Zhongguo Waijiao (China's Diplomacy)*. Beijing: Shijie Zhishi Chubanshe, 1997–2006.

Fourth, the formation of international production chains has provided the bond between China and Southeast Asia, especially the more developed ones. Increasingly, Southeast Asia began producing intermediates for final assembling in China before exporting to developed markets. As a result, in recent years, China has been importing more from Southeast Asia than exporting, allowing Southeast Asia to run a large trade surplus. China shoulders most of the blame for its trade surplus with the United States and EU, part of which can be attributed to Southeast Asia's trade surplus with China.

In this period China had embarked on a host of initiatives that aimed to create closer political and economic relations with Southeast Asia. First, China deepened its multilateral political ties with Southeast Asia, especially through ASEAN. Institutional mechanisms were developed to facilitate China-ASEAN cooperation. At the first informal summit of China and ASEAN (10+1) in December 1997 a joint statement was issued, announcing their partnership in good neighbourliness and mutual trust for the coming century. By early 1997 five parallel institutions (committees or official consultation) had been set up. China also participated in a series of ASEAN consultative meetings, including the ASEAN Regional Forum (ARF), the Post Ministerial Conferences (PMC) 9+1 and 9+10, the Joint Cooperation Committee (JCC) Meeting, the ASEAN-China Senior Officials Meeting (SOM), and the ASEAN-China Business Council Meeting. Second, progress had been made in China's bilateral relations with ASEAN members. In 1999 and 2000 China signed framework agreement of cooperation with all ASEAN states. China and Vietnam signed the Treaty on Land Border in December 1999 and an agreement demarcating maritime territory in the Gulf of Tonkin in 2000. Third, China made efforts to defuse tensions over sensitive issues with ASEAN, especially the South China Sea. In March 2000 China and ASEAN officials discussed their draft Codes of Conduct for the South China Sea and subsequently signed the Declaration on the Conduct of Parties in the South China Sea in November 2002. Fourth, China pushed ahead with a free trade area (FTA) with ASEAN, or China-ASEAN FTA (CAFTA). China raised the idea of an FTA at the ASEAN+3 Summit in November 2000. It made a formal proposal for an FTA one year later. Two years after its initial proposal the Framework Agreement on ASEAN-China Comprehensive Economic Cooperation was signed at the ASEAN-China Summit. An FTA will be established for China and six original ASEAN states in 2010 and for China and Cambodia, Laos, Myanmar and Vietnam by 2015. The early harvest programme, agreed initially in 2002, finalised in 2003 and commenced in 2004, cut China's tariffs on agricultural products from ASEAN.[24]

Strategic Partnership on Multilateralism and Good Neighbourliness: 2003 to Present

When President Hu and Premier Wen came to power in March 2003, they had to deal with the Severe Acute Respiratory Syndrome (SARS) outbreak and the temporary weakening of China-Southeast Asia ties. Within a few months they had the epidemic under control and managed to stabilise bilateral ties. In late 2003 they also formulated the well-publicised peaceful rise strategy. China has also undertaken a flurry of initiatives to forge strategic partnership with Southeast Asia.

In early 2003, ASEAN-China ties were interrupted briefly by the spread of SARS. ASEAN states felt that China did not respond openly and effectively to the epidemic in its initial months. As a result, the disease was transmitted by travellers from southern China to Southeast Asia, infecting 239 people and killing 21. The epidemic caused mass panic in the region and severely disrupted the service industries in the region. It also caused a downturn in ASEAN-China relations. In mid April 2003, the Hu-Wen leadership in China dismissed incompetent senior officials and swiftly mobilised the nation to fight the epidemic. Beijing also started to cooperate closely with Southeast Asian nations in anti-epidemic efforts. In April 2003, Premier Wen took his first overseas trip since assuming office to attend the special ASEAN summit on SARS in Bangkok. He acknowledged the limits in China's early anti-epidemic

---

[24]Saw, Sheng, and Chin, eds. *ASEAN-China Relations: Realities and Prospects*, pp. 2–4. See also postings on http://www.aseansec.org.

efforts and pledged cooperation.[25] By June the disease was under control and China's relations with Southeast Asia were back on track.

In October 2003, Premier Wen attended the 7th ASEAN-China summit in Bali. The historical Joint Declaration on the Strategic Partnership for Peace and Prosperity defined bilateral ties as strategic, yet non-exclusive. China also signed the key ASEAN security protocol, i.e., the Treaty of Amity and Cooperation, pledging its compliance with sovereignty and equality. China was the first non-ASEAN power to sign the treaty. This was also China's first strategic partnership with a regional organisation, marking a new era in ASEAN-China cooperative partnership. China also proposed to look at the feasibility of an East Asian free trade area.[26]

In late 2003, China proclaimed it would follow the path of peaceful rise. Zheng Bijian, then Executive Vice President of the Central Party School of the Chinese Communist Party (CCP), proposed the idea of peaceful rise at the Bo'ao Forum in Hainan, China in November 2003. Premier Wen Jiabao reiterated the concept on his visit to the United States in December 2003. The notion of peaceful rise has been hailed as President Hu's international strategy for China.[27] As stated, peaceful rise was derived from Deng's notion of "peace and development" as the trend of the time as well as Jiang's "a responsible big power". It was also a long sought after and carefully constructed response to the China threat argument enunciated by the West.

---

[25]For China's SARS management in the initial months and the change afterward, see Hongyi Lai, "Local Management of SARS in China: Guangdong and Beijing," in John Wong and Zheng Yongnian, eds. *The SARS Epidemic: Challenges to China's Crisis Management*, New Jersey and London: World Scientific, 2004, pp. 77–98. For China's interaction with ASEAN in anti-epidemic issues, see Hongyi Lai, "Regional Cooperation in Preventing Epidemics: China and ASEAN," in John Wong, Zou Keyuan and Zeng Huanquan, eds. *China-ASEAN Relations: Economic and Legal Dimensions.* Singapore: World Scientific Press, 2006, pp. 59–73.

[26]*Zhongguo Waijiao (China's Diplomacy).* Beijing: Shijie Zhishi Chubanshe, 2004, pp. 51–2; 312–13; Saw, Sheng, and Chin, eds. *ASEAN-China Relations: Realities and Prospects*, pp. 3, 7.

[27]Zheng Yongnian and Tok Sow Keat, "China's Peaceful Rise (I): Hu-Wen's Core Foreign Policy Strategy," pp. 1, 3–4.

The concept was received quite positively around the world. Nevertheless, it had given rise to two concerns in China. First, the one-sided emphasis on peaceful diplomacy might have given the wrong impression that China would renounce, under all conditions, the use of force against Taiwan's independence, thus emboldening independence forces in Taiwan.[28] Second, "rise" was too strong a word. It could arouse the deep-rooted uneasiness of other countries about China. To allay these two concerns, the Chinese authority replaced "peaceful rise" with "peaceful development" ostensibly in 2004, emphasising China's preoccupation with domestic development and its appreciation of external peace for that purpose. This shift was pronounced in Premier Wen's speech at the Bo'ao Forum in November 2003 that China pursued peace, development, cooperation and prosperity in Asia.

Thereafter, China continued to make impressive advances in its multilateral and bilateral relations with ASEAN states. First, ASEAN-China ties continue to flourish. At the ASEAN-China summit in Vientiane in November 2004, the Plan of Action to Implement the Joint Declaration on ASEAN-China Strategic Partnership for Peace and Prosperity was issued; ASEAN and China also agreed to put in place dispute resolution mechanisms. Both sides also signed a memorandum to build an information superhighway in the Greater Mekong River Region. At the ASEAN-China summit in Kuala Lumpur in November 2005, Premier Wen announced that China would provide $3.3 billion in low interest loans and favourable export credits for buyers in the following three years; this was one-third of China's total loan commitment to developing nations.

Second, ASEAN-China cooperation in formerly sensitive areas is also making progress. In 2004, China and the Philippines concluded a pact on joint ocean seismic work in the South China Sea. In 2004 and 2005 ASEAN and China continued with their discussion on the implementation of Codes of Conduct for the South China Sea. In 2005 a joint working group for that purpose was established.

Third, China has also made conscious efforts in providing generous aid to disaster-struck Southeast Asian nations. In the aftermath of the

---

[28]Goldstein, *Rising to the Challenge*, pp. 191–92.

Indian Ocean tsunami in December 2004, China offered assistance in material and cash worth $2.68 million. It also dispatched medical and rescue teams to Indonesia, and by March 2005, China had provided a total of $1.5 billion in aid to tsunami-stricken countries.

Fourth, there have been more frequent leadership exchanges between China and ASEAN members since 2004. In 2004, China received a significant number of leaders from Southeast Asia. They included Malaysian Prime Minister Abdullah Ahmad Badawi, Philippine President Gloria Macapagal-Arroyo, Thai Prime Minister Thaksin Shinawatra, Myanmar Prime Minister Khin Nyunt, Cambodian Prime Minister Hun Sen and Brunei Sudan. In 2005, Singaporean Prime Minister Lee Hsien Loong and Thai Prime Minister Thaksin visited China. In the same year, President Hu visited Brunei, Indonesia, the Philippines and Vietnam while the chairman of China's parliament Wu Bangguo visited Malaysia and Singapore and Premier Wen visited Malaysia. In 2006 Indonesian President Susilo Bambang Yudhoyono visited China. ASEAN leaders also attended the ASEAN-China commemorative summit in Nanning in 2006 where Premier Wen called for the deepening of cooperation within existing frameworks while strengthening social exchanges.

Overall Observations

The realignment of big powers and China's domestic reform have created a sea change in China's relations with Southeast Asia. When faced with an imminent Soviet threat, China sought détente with the US and a loose anti-Soviet alliance in the early 1970s. This strategic realignment continued right up till 1989. In the post-1989 period, China occasionally clashed with the West over human rights, Taiwan, and intrusion of sovereignty. Incidents included the West's sanctions and hostilities against China during the 1989-96 period, the NATO bombing of the Chinese embassy in 1999 and the US spy plane's landing in China's Hainan in 2001. Nevertheless, China managed to maintain a working relationship with the US. Improved Sino-American ties enabled Southeast Asia, especially Malaysia, Thailand, the Philippines, Indonesia and Singapore, to set up and develop ties with China between 1972 and 1989, and to expand their cooperation after 1989.

A more important cause for continual improvement in Southeast Asia-China relations has been China's economic reform and domestic development. Since 1978 China's leaders have been committed to the strategic goal of elevating the nation's status to that of a middle-income country. To achieve this goal, China has embarked peaceful diplomacy as its strategic course. China recognises the importance of maintaining an amicable relationship with this region where strategic sea lanes are located (the Straits of Malacca). Over the years, Southeast Asia has become an increasingly important source for China's FDI and trade, as well as inspiration for China's development and governance.

China and ASEAN also have quite a few things in common, in particular, the principle of non-interference in domestic affairs. This principle served China well when it is occasionally at odds with the West over human rights violation in events such as the Tianamen incident. The improvement in Sino-American relations since 1997 has further provided an amicable environment for closer ASEAN-China ties. China reciprocated Southeast Asia's good will by offering considerable assistance during and after the Asian financial crisis in 1997.

Closer economic ties with China have also dramatically altered Southeast Asia's perception of China. China is no longer perceived as a backward and unpredictable big power. It is now increasingly viewed as an economic dynamo, an engine of growth for the region and a land of opportunities as well as a benign big power.

The above factors, especially China's need for external peace and economic development, altogether explain the stream of initiatives and unprecedented collaboration between China and ASEAN in the last decade such as the signing of an FTA and the Declaration on the Conduct of Parties in the South China Sea.

China's economic development and smooth ascendance is contingent on its building peaceful ties with its neighbouring regions. China can be expected to continue with its strategy of peaceful rise for years to come. Its relations with ASEAN will remain stable, and it will search for solutions to defuse possible conflicts. ASEAN can reap maximum peace dividends through encouraging and engaging a peacefully rising China. While some issues may require skilful management, the cooperative efforts between China and ASEAN can result in an endurable strategic partnership that is anticipated to continue well into the new century.

China's Peaceful Rise and Its Political and Security Implications for Southeast Asia

Sheng Lijun

The rise of a major power certainly has political, security and economic implications. How nations perceived these implications and adopt accommodating or countering strategies is determined by their national interest. Take ASEAN-China relation for example, even though it has improved considerably for the past 15 years, most ASEAN nations, especially the original ASEAN 5 — Indonesia, Malaysia, Philippines, Singapore and Thailand — still maintain robust relations with the West and the United States. This shows that some ASEAN nations still have reservation about a rising China and is preventing the region's strategic balance from being tipped from the West to China. This paper attempts to understand this development by providing a detailed study of China's economic relations and exchanges with ASEAN and the United States' policy towards China in the region. It will also discuss the future of China-ASEAN relations.

China's Investment in ASEAN Is Still Small

Despite the huge bilateral trade volume with ASEAN, China's investment in the region is still very small. Therefore, its influence in ASEAN should not be exaggerated. For instance, at the end of 2004, China's accumulated investment in ASEAN, as registered in China's Ministry of Commerce, was US$1.2 billion (compared with US$38.2 billion of ASEAN's investment in China) compromising only about

8 percent of total overseas investment by Chinese companies.[1] This is a fraction of American investment in Southeast Asia which stood at US$85.4 billion. From 1995 to 2003, China's investment in ASEAN comprised only 0.3 percent of the total foreign investment in ASEAN, in sharp comparison to about 30 percent for European Union (EU), 17 percent for the United States and 13 percent for Japan.[2] If unregistered Chinese investments in the region were to be included, the figure is still likely to be small.

Furthermore, China's total investment to ASEAN countries has so far been dwarfed by that from both Japan and the United States. According to China's State Council and Ministry of Commerce, by the end of 2004, China's accumulated overseas investment (including investments by both the government and companies) was US$44.8 billion, 75 percent of which (or US$33.4 billion) went to Asia.[3] Of the amount, about 70 percent went to Hong Kong and the remaining to other Asian economies, including ASEAN.[4] Of this 30 percent, if

---

[1]These figures are from China's Ministry of Commerce. Also see "*Zhongguo qiye touzi dongmeng shichang cunzai wenti ji duice fengxi*" [Chinese Companies Invest in ASEAN Markets: Analysis of Problems and Policies], in China's official China-ASEAN FTA website, http://www.cafta.org.cn/shshshow1.asp?zs_id=32839 (12 November 2005). "*Zhongguo-Dongmeng touzi, laowu hezuo qude jingzhan*" [China and ASEAN: Progress in Investment and Labour Service Cooperation] in ibid., http://www.cafta.org.cn/shshshow1.asp?zs_id=33926, (14 January 2006). This article put the officially registered investment by Chinese companies in ASEAN as low as US$1.14 billion.

[2]These figures are from ASEAN Secretariat, quoted from ibid. Also see "*Dongnanya: Zhongguo qiye 'zouchuqu' de zhongdian diqu*" [Southeast Asia: A Key Area for Chinese Companies 'Going Out'", *Guoji gongcheng yu laowu* [International Projects and Labour] (China's Ministry of Commerce), no. 10, 2005, quoted from China's official website of China-ASEAN-FTA, http://www.cafta.org.cn/shshshow1.asp?zs_id=34530, (5 March 2006).

[3]The News Office, the State Council of the PRC, "*Zhongguo de heping fazhan daolu*" [China's Peaceful Development Road], *Renmin Ribao* (overseas edition), 23 December 2005, http://www.people.com.cn/GB/paper39/16473/1452590.html. These figures are also available from the official website of China's Ministry of Commerce, http://www.mofcom.gov.cn.

[4]Ibid.

Chinese investments in North Korea, Japan and other Asian countries were excluded, what is left for ASEAN is not much. In addition, in 2004 alone, China's overseas investment in Asia was US$3 billion or about 55 percent of its total overseas investment. But the lion's share (US$2.6 billion) went to Hong Kong. Only US$370 million went to other Asian economies and among which US$62 million headed for Indonesia and US$48 million for Singapore.[5]

Besides investment, China's economic aid to ASEAN countries is still very small compared to that from Japan and the United States. This further questioned just how influential China is in this region. Although China's government economic aid and government investment to ASEAN countries have been increasing steadily since 2005, particularly to Indonesia, Cambodia, the Philippines and Myanmar, they still could not match those from developed countries. Furthermore, the bulk of Chinese aid is slated for North Korea, Africa and Latin American countries. As a result, little remains for ASEAN countries. Government investment in ASEAN countries will increase but Chinese companies continue to prefer to invest domestically for various reasons including higher profit and lower risk. The result is a massive increase in China's trade with other countries, but far more modest increase in investment overseas by Chinese companies.

The question of how China will eventually use its huge foreign reserve will also play a role in identifying the magnitude of China's rise in Southeast Asia. China's foreign reserve is growing fast, exceeding US$1 trillion by October 2006. It is still not clear at this moment whether China will continue to keep the huge foreign reserve or to spend it for domestic needs or overseas investments. Even if Beijing decided to spend it overseas, it remains to be seen whether it will be used to purchase shares of those well-established Western multinational companies (MNCs) or for its mergers and acquisition (M&A) companies in developed countries for the acquisition of technology, management or marketing expertise that China badly needed, or to use it as Official Development Assistance (ODA) to developing countries. If it is the

---

[5]Ibid.

latter, will China's ODA focus on Africa or South America for acquiring energy resources or on ASEAN countries for strategic purposes?

China-ASEAN Bilateral Trade

While the prospect is not yet clear, what features clearly and prominently in China-ASEAN economic relations so far is not investment and economic aid but the rapid growth in bilateral trade. Growing at an annual rate of more than 20 percent from 1990 to 2003, it was over US$100 billion in 2004. Today, ASEAN is China's fourth biggest trade partner, and China the fifth biggest partner of ASEAN.[6]

However, the huge trade figures can be deceiving. First, most of the goods exported from China to ASEAN are from the processing industry, mostly owned by foreign companies in China. In fact, in 2004, foreign companies comprised 77 percent of the top 200 exporters in China and 62 percent of the top 500 importers.[7] According to official figures, in 2005, 55 percent (US$416 billion) of China's total exports in 2005 (US$762 billion) were from the processing industry.[8] Furthermore, in the same year, the trade volume from these foreign companies in China reached US$831.7 billion (an increase of more than 25 percent from the year before), which comprised about 60 percent of China's total trade.[9] From 2000–2004, the value of all exports by foreign companies

---

[6]"ASEAN Centre of Contemporary Chinese Studies in offing", *People's Daily on Line* (English Edition), 27 August 2005. "Hu Jintao: Zhongguo yaxi'an nianmaoyi'e wunian nei kepo 2000 yi meiyuan" [Hu Jintao: China-ASEAN Annual Trade May Reach US$200 in Five Years], *Lianhe Zaobao* [United Morning News] (Singapore), 27 April 2005.

[7]"*Maoyi daguo anran shice, zhongguo wehe meiyu dingjiaquan?*" [A Trade Power under Challenge: Why China Cannot Decide the Price?] *China Daily* (Chinese edition) (Beijing), 19 August 2005. According to China Minister of commerce Bo Xilai, these foreign companies accounted for 58 percent of China's total export in 2004. See report on his press conference on 11 April 2006, http://boxilai.mofcom.gov.cn/aarticle/activi ties/200604/20060401877307.html

[8]See the annual report by China's Ministry of Commerce, *Zhongguo duiwai maoyi xingshi baogao* [China's Foreign Trade], 2006, available at http://www.cafta.org.cn/shshshow1.asp?zs_id=35868.

[9]Ibid.

in China increased from US$119.4 billion to US$338.6 billion, an increase from 48 percent to 57 percent of China's total exports. At the same time, their imports increased from US$117.3 billion in 2000 to US$324.6 billion in 2004, an increase of 52 percent or about 58 percent of China's total imports. As a result, their total trade volume during the period registered an annual growth of more than 50 percent from US$236.7 billion in 2000 to US$663.2 billion in 2004.

Second, the figures for Chinese exports were flawed by heavy double counting as China accounted for only a fraction of the value of the finished products. As a result, it could also have contributed to the inflation of China-ASEAN trade figures. Double counting is estimated to account for as high as 30 percent of the total trade between China and ASEAN. This came as one US report put the profit rate for China at 17 cents for every US dollar China exported. One Chinese study in 2003 shows that China produced 75 percent of the toys in the world, but only retains 1/70 of the total profit.[10] The New York Times in 2006 reported that "the biggest beneficiary" of China's increased export is not China:

> A Barbie doll (China exported to the United States) costs US$20, but China only gets about 35 cents of that. Because so many different hands in different places touch a particular product, you might as well throw away the trade figures (of China's exports).[11]

Third, the sharp increase in China-ASEAN trade could also be caused by intra-industrial trade within and between foreign companies or MNCs in China and Southeast Asia as well as entrepot trade. Intra-industry trade can spur innovation and competition, especially between different MNCs (much of it between different international companies or between subsidiaries and headquarters of the same international company). The China-Singapore trade makes up the lion's share of the China-ASEAN trade. Of this, entrepot trade accounts for 46 percent of China's export to Singapore and 40 percent of Singapore's export to

---

[10]News Report, China CCTV Channel 4, 17 January 2003.
[11]David Barboza, "Some Assembly Needed: China as Asia Factory", New York Times, 9 February 2006.

China.[12] That is, a large part of China's trade with ASEAN ends up in Western consumer markets. Apparently, Western consumer markets have tremendous influence over China's foreign trade especially before China can change its current export-oriented development strategy to a domestic-consumption-driven one.

Fourth, Chinese companies are unable to establish themselves in ASEAN countries to compete in their markets. Firstly, they are mainly medium and small companies without the huge funds necessary to effectively compete with the foreign companies, which are already firmly established in ASEAN markets. Secondly, the Chinese companies are not coordinated and well-integrated with ASEAN markets, not even among themselves. They were "pushed" to "go overseas" by the individual provinces or cities where they are located. As a result, there is no strong nation-wide overseas strategy for each industry. Chinese companies in Southeast Asia and in other places often compete with other Chinese companies from other provinces rather than compete with foreign companies in the region. Furthermore, most of the Chinese companies have insufficient knowledge of ASEAN markets.[13] Moreover, they often operate on a "hit-and-run" fashion for immediate one time profit at the expense of their overall long-term interest and reputation, thus rendering them vulnerable to the competition of both foreign and local companies. For example, they often flood ASEAN markets with cheap and low quality Chinese products such as garments and textiles. Chinese companies also could not compete in the upper tier of the economic ladder. Thirdly, only Chinese companies from Yunnan Province and Guangxi Autonomous Region have the strongest enthusiasm to invest and penetrate the ASEAN market. The better-developed coastal provinces focus on Western markets and only

---

[12]Xu Changwen, "*Zhongguo yu xinjiapo jingmao hezuo kuaisu fazhan*" [China and Singapore: Rapid Development in Their Economic and Trade Cooperation], *Zhongguo Jingji Shibao* [China Economic Times], 7 April 2006, available on http://www.cafta.org. cn/shshshow1.asp?zs_id=34930

[13]For details, see "*Yingxiang zhongguo yu dongmeng jingmao fazhan de yinsu ji duice*" [China and ASEAN Economic and Trade Development: Unfavourable Factors and Countermeasures], in China's official China-ASEAN FTA website, http://www.cafta. org.cn/shshshow1.asp?zs_id=33600 (19 December 2005).

look to ASEAN when they are unable to expand further in Western markets. In 2001, for example, trade with ASEAN comprised the largest portion of the foreign trade of Guangxi and Yunnan (36 percent). But Guangxi and Yunnan's trade with ASEAN only totalled US$1.6 billion and made up only about 4 percent of China' total trade with ASEAN (US$41.6 billion). Guangdong Province traded US$15.4 billion with ASEAN countries, which made up 37 percent of China' total trade with ASEAN in that year.[14] However, for Guangdong, China's top exporter, it was only about 9 percent its total foreign trade.[15] Its focus is on the US, Japan and other Western markets. It is also the same for other developed Chinese provinces and cities such as Shanghai whose trade with ASEAN comprised only 8 percent of its total foreign trade in the same year.[16] This shows that large competitive Chinese companies generally do not look to ASEAN as major markets and essential trade partners, but as supplementary markets and partners. The majority of them are engaged in trading, not manufacturing in ASEAN countries. As high as 90 percent of China's exports to the world in this trading are through foreign companies or MNCs in the form of Original Equipment Manufacturers (OEM). To make matter worse, Chinese companies lack in-depth research and information of developments in the many ASEAN markets. A successful, deep and large-scale penetration of Chinese companies into Southeast Asia remains difficult at the moment.

Fourth, bilateral trade growth as a proportion of total trade is not as impressive as in absolute terms. For example, from 2000–2005, China's trade with ASEAN grew at an annual rate of well over 30 percent. However, China's total foreign trade also increased at an annual rate

---

[14]Shi Benzhi & Dai Jie, eds., *Lancangjiang-Meigonghe ciquyu hezuo yu zhongguo-dongmeng ziyou maoyiqu jianshe* [Lancang River-Greater Mekong sub-Regional Cooperation and the Building of China-ASEAN FTA] (Beijing: China Commerce and Trade Press, 2005), pp. 239, 254. However, according to statistics from Guangdong Province, the total trade of that year was US$14.958 billion.

[15]Guangdong Provincial Statistics Bureau, *Guangdong tongji nianjian 2003* [Statistics Yearbook of Guangdong Province 2003]. Beijing, China Statistics Press, 2003.

[16]*Shanghai duiwai jingji maoyi nianjian 2002* [Shanghai Yearbook of Foreign Economy and Trade 2002] and *Shanghai duiwai jingji maoyi tongji nianjian 2002* [Shanghai Statistics Yearbook of Foreign Economy and Trade 2002].

of over 30 percent in the same period. In other words, this growth in China-ASEAN trade can well be said to be a normal one, especially when one considers that bilateral trade between the two sides started from a very low volume and foreign companies in China accounted for about 61 percent of China's trade with ASEAN in 2005. This trade comprised about 8 percent of China's total foreign trade in 2000,[17] rising to nearly 11 percent in 2004,[18] before dropping to 9 percent in 2005.[19] So, there is growth, but not spectacular growth, considering that China's total trade with Asian countries reached US$665 billion in 2004 compared with its US$101 billion trade with ASEAN in that year.[20] Asia comprised about 58 percent of China's total foreign trade in 2004, while trade with ASEAN was about 11 percent.[21] In 2005 China-ASEAN trade grew by 23 percent to US$130.4 billion,[22] in comparison with previous high growth rates (43 percent for 2003 and 40 percent for 2004). In the same year, China's total foreign trade stood at US$1.5 trillion, an increase of 23 percent from 2004.[23] China's trade with India grew by 38 percent[24] and its trade with Russia grew by 37 percent.[25] So the

---

[17]*Forging Closer ASEAN-China Economic Relations in the Twenty-First Century*, a report submitted by the ASEAN-China Expert Group on Economic Cooperation, October 2001, p. 1, http://www.asean.or.id/newdata/Asean-chi.pdf

[18]The author's own calculation.

[19]"2010 *nian zhongguo-dongmeng maoyi'e jiangda 2000 yi meiyuan*" [China-ASEAN Trade will Reach US$200 by 2010] *Xin Jing Bao* [*The Beijing News*] (Beijing), 10 January 2006, from http://www.cafta.org.cn/shshshow1.asp?zs_id=33882 (2006/1/11)

[20]"ASEAN Center of Contemporary Chinese Studies in Offing", *Renmin Ribao*, 27 August 2005. "Hu Jintao: China-ASEAN Annual Trade May Reach US$200 Billion in Five Years", *Lianhe Zaobao*, 27 April 2005.

[21]The State Council of the PRC, "Zhongguo de heping fazhan daolu" [China's Peaceful Development Road], op. cit.

[22]Xinhua News Agency, 17 March 2006, cited in China's official China-ASEAN FTA website, http://www.caexpo.org/gb/news/trade/t20060317_58704.html

[23]See the annual report by China's Ministry of Commerce, *Zhongguo duiwai maoyi xingshi baogao* [China's Foreign Trade], 2006, available at http://www.cafta.org.cn/shshshow1.asp?zs_id=35868

[24]Paranjoy Guha Thakurta, "China Could Overtake US's India Trade", *Asia Times* (Bangkok), 15 March 2006.

[25]Xinhua News Agency, 17 March 2006, http://news.xinhuanet.com/world/2006-03/17/content_4312378.htm. Their two-way trade for 2005 was US$29.1 billion.

growth of China-ASEAN trade in 2005 (23 percent) was below average. Viewed from the ASEAN side, the same situation exists. Take China's largest ASEAN trade partner Singapore for example.[26] In 2005, its trade with China as at S$67.1 billion dwarfed that of many other ASEAN countries. Nevertheless, this figure is not large compared with Singapore's total foreign trade of S$716 billion that year.[27]

There is no intention to deny the fast growth of trade and China's fast rise in Southeast Asia, but would like to alert readers of the danger of accepting trade figures without proper perspective and the danger of exaggerating China's political influence in the region through the exaggeration of these trade figures to create a "China threat".

China's trade with ASEAN will continue to grow. Even if it reaches US$200 billion by 2010 as both sides anticipate, this volume will likely be in a similar (or a bit higher) proportion to China's total foreign trade. What is more, with the massive entrants of MNCs into China following its entry into WTO at the end of 2001, the proportion of foreign components in China's trade with ASEAN will continue to increase prominently and may increase from the current 61 percent. Then, the potential increase in China's trade with ASEAN, even if it reaches US$200 billion by 2010, should be read as mainly the increase of those foreign companies, especially MNCs, in China.

The social basis for a rising China in Southeast Asia to transform the regional strategic landscape is still weak. China's relationship with many ASEAN countries remains mainly at the governmental level (such as frequent exchange of visits by their leaders) and has not penetrated deeply and substantively to the middle and lower levels of the society. China has not yet succeeded in establishing many channels and mechanisms of cooperation at various levels (from the top to the grass-root levels) of the ASEAN countries, which will lead to strong political, economic, strategic, social, cultural and religious bond between them.

---

[26]Singapore has been China's largest ASEAN trade partner for many years, though occasionally overtaken by Malaysia.

[27]*Straits Times*, 18 January 2006, p. 1. Total China-ASEAN trade in 2004 was US$109.9 billion.

China's Rise and the United States in Southeast Asia

All the aforementioned illustrate that despite China's recent rise in Southeast Asia, an active and evolving regional balance of power still remains; the author does not see a Chinese dominance in the region presently or in the near future. The United States, though watchful of China's rise in Southeast Asia, does not see the urgency to shift its defence and diplomatic gravity massively to Southeast Asia. This is largely because of the following reasons.

First, the US is still engaged in global anti-terrorism war. Global terrorism and asymmetrical warfare pose a completely new challenge to the United States, as its forces have always been structured for a general war with conventional powers. This time, Washington is engaged in a "shadow war" where the opponent is elusive. Reconfiguring the forces and operations doctrine to handle this "shadow war" is a must for Washington and it will take both time and huge resources. What is more, the war against terrorism itself is a long one as stated by former US. Defence Secretary Donald Rumsfeld. He said, "It strikes me that this is not a conventional war that starts and ends with a signing ceremony on a battleship. It's more like the Cold War."[28] This long war against the "shadow opponent" will dearly tap on US' strategic resources that would otherwise be used to maintain its global primacy vis-à-vis rising powers. As a result, a real victory now is not about how many powers to defeat, but is about the maintenance and acquisition of strategic resources.

Second, being tied down by the need to conserve its strategic resources in its war against terrorism, the United States could not significantly alter its East Asian strategy to contain China. Instead of focussing on containing China's influence in less strategically important small countries, Washington aims to strengthen its ties with its allies and big powers in regions such as Japan, Australia and India. This is to seek a favourable balance of power instead of absolute dominance and to astride important sea-lanes.

---

[28]See remarks by Rumsfeld at the 5th Shangri La Dialogue in Singapore, *Today* (Singapore), 5 June 2006, p. 1.

Third and more importantly, because of its weak economic, political and social basis in the region as analysed aforesaid, China, as it appears to US, cannot overturn the regional balance of power overnight. Because of the political, religious, cultural and ethnical complexity of the region, it is always more difficult to set up a binding and effective regional organisation dominated by one power than to break or sabotage it by driving a wedge. So long as China was unable set up an exclusive and powerful power block in East Asia to tilt the regional balance of power, Washington does not have to worry. Even if United States cannot set up something in the region, it can always break the power block easily. And this may partly explain why Washington is not alarmed, though concerned of, by China's rise in the region.

As for ASEAN, China's rise appears to be an opportunity. Strategically, ASEAN pursue a policy of constructive engagement with all the powers; the engagement of China in this region and China's political backing enhance ASEAN's status as the primary driving force in regional affairs. A rising China, with its booming economy, provides many niche markets inside China for ASEAN countries. From December 2001 to September 2005, China's annual imports stood at an average of US$500 billion and created about 10 million employment opportunities for other countries and regions. China's imports are expected to reach US$1 trillion by 2010[29] and China-ASEAN trade could exceed US$200 billion by 2010.[30] This huge demand for Chinese imports provides many trade opportunities for ASEAN countries, which, in recent years, have benefitted from a huge trade surplus with China at nearly US$20 billion a year. What is encouraging for ASEAN is that Beijing is prepared to tolerate such a huge trade deficit to assure good relations with ASEAN. Over the past few years, ASEAN's trade with China has exceeded its trade with other countries.

---

[29]The State Council of the PRC, *"Zhongguo de heping fazhan daolu"* [China's Peaceful Development Road], op. cit.
[30]"ASEAN Center of Contemporary Chinese Studies in offing", op. cit. "Hu Jintao: China-ASEAN Annual Trade May Reach US$200 in Five Years", op. cit.

Future Implications of China-ASEAN Relations

What are the implications of a fast rising China to ASEAN in the future? There will be more profound changes to China-ASEAN relations. Globalisation has affected China's economic development in three stages. The first stage is before 2001 when China joined the WTO. China's export-oriented strategy in this period was based on cheap labour and export of low value-added products at the lower tier of international economic chain.

Things started to change much faster with the set in of the second stage at the end of 2001 with the massive entrants of MNCs into China following its WTO accession. The massive flow-in of these MNCs into the Chinese market has three consequences: First, China's foreign trade volume has sharply increased from 2002. Trade volume between China and ASEAN soared. In fact, in 2003 and 2004 it increased by over 40 percent. Second, the MNCs brought with them not only FDI but also high technology and management expertise. Therefore, China's industry upgrading has been faster than ASEAN especially in the forthcoming third stage. This has significant implications for ASEAN-China relations. Third, with the MNCs flooding in, China's foreign reserve has grown very fast to exceed US$1 trillion by October 2006. As it does not make sense for China to keep such a huge foreign reserve especially when MNCs in China will continue to increase its export and generate more trade surplus and more foreign reserves for China. How China is going to spend the foreign reserves is obviously an economic issue that has profound political implications on its foreign relations. In the first two stages, China focussed on the export of goods, but in the third stage China may sooner or later start to export both goods and, significantly, capital as well, perhaps in the form of government loans and trade credit and M&A

In this stage too, the enormous effort by China to upgrade its industry and science and technology as well as the full operation of MNCs in China is likely to speed up China's industrial upgrading in the international economic chain, overtaking that of ASEAN countries. China will likely have much more surplus industrial capability, which it has little use for but to export to other developing countries, including ASEAN countries, in exchange for its much needed energy and resources. This, again, will have tremendous political implications for state-to-state relations between China and ASEAN. Therefore, in the third stage, which starts from now, many interesting and important changes will take place in China-ASEAN relations that need to be watched and studied carefully.

China-Myanmar Relations Since 1988

Li Chenyang

Of all the bilateral relations China has with ASEAN member states, China-Myanmar relations appear to be the most unique. This uniqueness was nurtured through the traditional *paukphaw* (brotherhood) between the two nations and after the formation of the Myanmar military regime in September 1988. After the Cold War, China started to pursue the strategy of establishing or re-establishing full bilateral relations with all ASEAN members. Despite the fact that China's cooperation with Myanmar in quite a few areas is not as deep and close as that with other member states, China is often the target of Western criticism for establishing a "special" relationship with Myanmar and hindering the democratisation process in Myanmar. This paper attempts to give an objective assessment and description of the nature and characteristics of China-Myanmar bilateral relations since 1988. It also studies how Myanmar's political landscape and regional influence shape the relationship and explores the direction China-Myanmar relationship might be heading in the coming years.

Political, Economic and Security Cooperation since 1988

To understand the nature of China-Myanmar relations, it is necessary to have an objective analysis of the political, economic and security cooperation between the two. Since the founding of the People's Republic of China, the two countries have maintained friendly ties except for the 1967–1970 period when they were briefly at odds with each other. What is noteworthy is that bilateral cooperation since 1988 has been deepened and broadened.

1. *Political Cooperation*

Political cooperation finds its expression both in the frequent exchange of visits by top leaders and in the mutual support over important issues, thus building a high level of mutual political trust. From September 1988, visits to China by Myanmar top leaders include General Saw Maung, Chairman of the State Law and Order Restoration Council (SLORC) in August 1991; General Than Shwe, Chairman of State Peace and Development Council (SPDC, formerly SLORC until November 1997) in January 1996 and January 2003; General Khin Nyunt (sacked as premier in October 2004) in July 2004, and General Soe Win (current premier) in November 2004, July 2005, November 2005, February 2006 and November 2006. Top Chinese leaders' visits to Myanmar include Premier Li Peng in October 1994 and President Jiang Zemin in December 2001. Special attention should be given to the first high ranking delegation led by SLORC's vice chairman and commander-in-chief of the army, Lt-general Than Shwe, to China in October 1989 after the military regime came to power and the visit by State Law and Order Restoration Council's Chairman General Saw Maung in October 1991. This was General Saw Maung's only official visit to China during his administration, a visit which somewhat saved China from any diplomatic embarrassment at that time.

Other important mutual visits were by Luo Gan, State Councilor and General Coordinator of China's State Council in January 1991; Qian Qichen, State Councilor and Foreign Minister in February 1993; Li Ruihuan, Chinese People Political Consultative Conference (CPPCC) Chairman in March 1997; Wu Banguo, Vice Premier in October 1997; Hu Jintao, Vice President in July 2000; Li Lanqing, Vice Premier in January 2003; Wu Yi, Vice Premier in March 2004, and Li Zhaoxing, Foreign Minister in July 2005. Myanmarese officials who visited China include General Khin Nyunt, State Peace and Development Council (SPDC) first secretary in September 1994, June 1999, June 2002 and January 2003; Tin Oo, SLORC second secretary in November 1994; General Maung Aye, SPDC Vice Chairman and Commander-in-Chief of the army in October 1996 and June 2000, and Lt-General Win Myin, SPDC third secretary in October 2000.

Apart from these mutual visits, the two countries keep close contact on the sideline of various multinational conferences when dealing with important global and regional affairs. Officials coordinate stances and assist each other over issues concerning national interest. Beijing also always opposed economic sanctions against Myanmar proposed either by the West or international organisations such as the International Labour Organisation (ILO). Furthermore, in many occasions, China refused to put the Myanmar issue on the United Nations Security Council (UNSC) agenda and veto any United Nations resolution on Myanmar. In return, Myanmar is very consistent in supporting the "One China policy".

In June 2000, to mark the 50th anniversary of the establishment of diplomatic ties, the two countries signed a Joint Declaration on the Framework of Future Bilateral Cooperation, setting goals and principles for the further development of bilateral ties in the 21st century.

2. Economic Cooperation

Much importance has also been placed on economic cooperation covering trade, investment, economic aid, loans and contracted projects. Since 1988, over 50 bilateral agreements and memorandum of understandings (MOUs) on economic cooperation have been concluded. Myanmar takes the development of economic relations with China as a very important factor in pushing Myanmar's economic modernisation. This is embodied in the formation of the Myanmar-China Economic Cooperation and Promotion Council of 12 cabinet ministers chaired by the then first secretary of SLORC. During President Jiang Zemin's visit in December 2001, the two sides agreed to place agriculture, human resources, natural resources and infrastructure development on the top of their cooperation agenda.

Myanmar-China bilateral trade grew rapidly after Myanmar launched its open-door policy in 1987. Within a year, bilateral trade volume doubled from US$100 million in 1987 to US$255 million in 1988. In the first half of the 1990s, bilateral trade continued to grow, reaching US$767 million in 1995. Bilateral trade however dipped from 1996 to 1999 largely due to the Asian financial crisis and the

Myanmar government's readjustment of its trade policy. Trade
picked up from 2000 to reach US$1.1 billion in 2004. Currently,
China is Myanmar's third largest trade partner after Singapore and
Thailand.

Yunnan Province's trade with Myanmar accounted for almost half
of Myanmar-China total trade volume but this share seems to be getting
smaller (see Table 1). China's exports to Myanmar are mainly electrical
appliances and machinery (ships, engineering and construction vehicles,
locomotives, farming machines, hydro-electrical apparatus, dock

Table 1. Myanmar's Trade with China and Yunnan (million US Dollars)

Year	Trade between Myanmar and China[A]		Trade between Myanmar and Yunnan Province[B]		B as % of A	B as % of Yunnan's Export plus Import
	Total	Growth %	Total	Growth %		
1991	39209	19.7	4071	–	10.38	7.4
1992	39031	−0.5	22537	453.6	57.74	33.6
1993	48953	25.4	38155	69.3	77.94	45.4
1994	51239	4.7	42042	10.2	82.05	31.3
1995	76740	49.8	49013	16.6	63.86	23.1
1996	65853	−14.2	36274	−26	55.08	17.62
1997	64349	−2.3	30477	−1.6	47.36	15.17
1998	58000	−9.9	38100	25	65.68	15.17
1999	50848	−12.3	29952	−21.4	58.90	18.05
2000	62100	22.1	36294	21.2	58.44	20.02
2001	63200	1.8	34873	−3.9	55.17	17.53
2002	86171	36.40	40678	16.6	47.20	18.27
2003	107700	25	49279	18.5	45.80	22.10
2004	114500	6.3	55136	11.9	48.20	14.7
2005	120933	5.6	63162	14.6	52.20	13.33
Jan. to Oct. 2006	115900	22.3	55733	5.9	48.10	10.99

Source: Ministry of Commerce of PRC, Department of Commerce of Yunnan Province.

equipment, sugar and textile-processing facilities), high-tech products, chemical products, textiles and medicines. Imports from Myanmar are timber, mineral and aquatic products. Under the China-ASEAN free trade agreement, China granted Myanmar a preferential policy of zero tariffs for 197 items, which increased Myanmar's tariff-free commodities items to China to 90 percent.

Since 1988, China provided Myanmar with considerable amount of aid and preferential loans and cancelled numerous debts. Statistics show that by 2005, China's total aid to Myanmar reached about US$100 million.[1] From 1991 to 2005, the Bank of China and China Import-Export Bank provided Myanmar with seller's credits worth over US$1 billion.[2] In 2006, China provided another US$85 million of loans to Myanmar to purchase two new oil-drillers. The two sides also signed an agreement that will see Beijing providing infrastructure loans to five Myanmar government departments. Chinese construction companies in Myanmar also have a large share in bilateral economic cooperation. By the end of 2002, Chinese construction companies had invested in more than 800 projects worth over US$2 billion.[3] By the end of 2005, the amount rose to nearly US$3.9 billion with a fulfilled turnover of US$2.2 billion[4].

Chinese investment in Myanmar was small during the late 1980s and the 1990s. However, the situation improved after the two sides signed the Agreement on the Protection of Investment by the Two Governments during President Jiang Zemin's visit to Myanmar in 2001. With the agreement, China's investment in Myanmar increased rapidly. According to the statistics of the Myanmar Investment Commission, as of May 2005, China invested 26 projects in Myanmar, totalling $194 million or about 1.4 percent of the overall investment in the country. China was the 11th largest investor in Myanmar in 2005, up from the

---

[1]Nyi Nyi Lwin, "Economic and Military Cooperation between China and Burma," September 2006, see http://www.narinjara.com/Reports/BReport.ASP.
[2]Yue Deming, "A Preliminary Study of Myanmar's China Policy in the Post-Cold War Era," Foreign Review, No. 4, December 2005, p. 58.
[3]http://www.farer.net.cn/Asia/city.asp?ID=45.
[4]http://www.fmprc.gov.cn/chn/wjb/zzjg/yzs/gjlb/1271/default.htm.

15th in 2002. China's investments are mainly in oil, natural gas, ore mining and manufacturing.[5]

According to some Chinese scholars' estimation, a huge number of minor investment projects that were not included in the Myanmar Investment Commission statistics already amounted to US$870 million back in 1994.[6] There was also a considerable amount of investment by some Chinese businesses in the ethnic-controlled special districts in border areas. By adding both official and unofficial figures, it is likely that the total Chinese investment in Myanmar is about US$1 billion.

3. Military and Security Cooperation

The international media perceived China as "an important military ally and arms supplier of Myanmar"[7] based on the multiple levels of Myanmar-China military relations. First, the foreign media reported a number of arms sale between the two sides in the 1990s. For instance, a US$1.4 billion deal was signed in October 1989 during SLORC Vice Chairman General Than Shwe's visit to China; this was followed by another deal of US$140 million in 1994.[8] The media also estimated that around 90 percent of Myanmar's weapons were supplied by China. In the 1990s alone, Chinese arms sale to Myanmar included 200 tanks, 288 fighter planes, 250 armoured carriers and other equipment such as artillery, naval vessels and missiles.[9]

Second, Myanmar's military personnel were trained by the People's Liberation Army (PLA). In October 1996, the foreign media reported that the PLA agreed to train 300 Myanmar navy and air force officers and set aside training camps at a Chinese military academy for the

---

[5]http://mm.mofcom.gov.cn/aarticle/jmxw/200607/20060702606645.html.

[6]*Far Eastern Economic Review*, 2 October 1994, p. 31.

[7]Rodney Tasker and Bertil Lintner, "Danger: Road Works Ahead," *Far Eastern Economic Review*, 21 December 2000, p. 26.

[8]D. M. Seekins, "Burma-China Relations: Playing with Fire," *Asian Survey*, Vol. 37, No. 6, p. 534. Denny Roy, *China's Foreign Relations*. Lanham, Maryland: Rowman & Littlefield Publishers, Inc, 1998, p. 174. Mary P. Callahan, "New Dragon or Still Dragging?" *Asian Survey*, Vol. 35, No. 2, February 1995, p. 206.

[9]Nyi Nyi Lwin, "Economic and Military Cooperation between China and Burma," September 2006, see http://www.narinjara.com/Reports/BReport.ASP.

exclusive use of the Myanmar trainees.[10] Third, foreign media noted that China has been helping Myanmar to modernise its military. One example was the PLA's decision to provide Myanmar with radar and sophisticated electronic facilities and to help them with the installation of equipment on some islands off Myanmar's southwest coast to upgrade its intelligence capability in the Indian Ocean. A second example was the transfer of military technology (chiefly naval-vessel building and repairing) to strengthen Myanmar's armament industry.

Fourth, the foreign media has also reported of close contact and frequent exchanges between the PLA and Myanmar's military. Some of the visits were made by Gen. He Qizong, Deputy Chief of Staff in November 1991; Gen. Chi Haotian, State Councilor and Defense Minister in July 1995; Gen. Zhang Wannian, Vice Chairman of Central Military Commission in April 1996; Gen. Fu Quanyou, Chief of Staff in April 2001; Gen. Wu Quanxu, Deputy Chief of Staff in December 2003; Gen. Ge Zhengfeng, Deputy Chief of Staff in December 2004, and Gen. Liang Guanglie, Chief of Staff in October 2006. On the Myanmar side, visits were made by Lt-Gen. Than Shwe, Vice Commander-in-Chief of the Armed Forces and Commander-in-Chief of the Army in October 1989; his successor Gen. Maung Aye in October 1996; Gen. Thura Shwe Mann, Joint Chief of Staff of the army, navy and air forces in December 2003 and Gen. Soe Win, SPDC first secretary of commander of the air defence force in July 2004. It was also reported that the two sides are expanding their military cooperation to include areas such as culture, education, health, tourism and the fight against drug trafficking.

Analysing China-Myanmar relations

China's relations with Myanmar are often perceived negatively by many foreign government agencies, academics and international organisations (including Non-Government Organisations). This paper will present a different perspective by analysing some fundamental issues of China-Myanmar relations.

---

[10]Peter W. Rodman, "China Woos Burma," *International Herald Tribune*, 30 May 1997.

1. China's Objectives in Pursuing China-Myanmar Relations

China aims to be a responsible stakeholder in the post-Cold War world economic and political arena. One of China's neighbours, Myanmar has been under the control of the military junta since 1988, causing worldwide denouncement of its anti-democracy activities and violation of domestic human rights. China keeps close relations with the military junta based on its non-interference policy, which however gave rise to some critical arguments.

China's motives in developing relations with Myanmar are clear. Firstly, after adopting the open-door policy in 1978, one of Beijing's major tasks is to normalise diplomatic relations and to ensure a peaceful environment with its peripheries. Given the fact that China and Myanmar share a common borderline of more than 2,200 kilometres, China is unlikely to be hostile to Myanmar. Secondly, China's foreign policies are in line with the Five Principles of Peaceful Co-Existence and would not change even in Myanmar's case. Thirdly, Myanmar is important to China's domestic economic development in terms of its geographical location and affluent natural resources. American scholar Jared Genser argues that China's two major motives in developing relations with Myanmar concerns natural resources and security.[11] Myanmar is a key economic partner for China's southwest provinces especially Yunnan as well as a passage linking Southwest China, Mainland Southeast Asia and South Asian countries. It is also a land bridge connecting Southwest China with Indian Ocean and even with African and European markets. Strategically Myanmar can play a role in China's presence in the Indian Ocean and its long-term "two ocean" strategies. Myanmar is therefore part and parcel of China's grand strategic design to achieve its overall goal of becoming a great power in the 21st century[12]. Myanmar's role in China's national security could be

---

[11]Jared Genser, "China's Role in the World: The China-Burma Relationship," A testimony to US-China Economic and Security Review Commission. 3 August 2006. http://www.uscc.gov/hearings/2006hearings/written_testimonies/06_08_3_4wrts/06_08_3_4_genser_jared_statement.php.

[12]Poon Kim Shee, "The Political Economy of China-Myanmar Relations: Strategic and Economic Dimensions," Ritsumeikan Annual Review of International Studies, The International Studies Association of Ritsumeikan University, 2002, p. 51.

seen from the Second World War during which the Yunnan-Myanmar Highway became a significant supply line. China is, however, unlikely to consider Myanmar as a strategic pawn in its potential confrontation with other great powers or a satellite state. So far there is no evidence that China is keen in making the country its economic and military colony[13].

China's effort in developing relations with Myanmar neither obstructs integration of Southeast Asia nor alienates Myanmar from regional integration. In other words, given the fact that China-ASEAN relations are far more important than China-Myanmar relations to China, China-Myanmar relations are unlikely to influence China-ASEAN relations as a whole. Some scholars thus argue that since 2000, China's Myanmar policy might be well evaluated under the frameworks China-ASEAN Free Trade Area (CAFTA), ASEAN plus One (China), ASEAN plus Three (China, Japan and South Korea) as well as China-ASEAN economic integration.[14] Singapore and Thailand are worried that if Myanmar became China's new passage of oil and goods transport it might divert commercial shipping away from the Straits of Malacca and the proposed Kra Canal. The fact is, with China's robust economic growth and sea transport as the most important way in modern times, there may not be a reduction in China's external trade in oil and goods via the Straits of Malacca even if there is a new trade passage to the Indian Ocean via Myanmar. From the long term perspective, China is not against the construction of the Kra Canal.

2. Is China-Myanmar Relation Particular or Normal?

Normal state to state relation is based on mutual benefit with each party moderating its policy towards the counterpart in accordance with its own state interest, instead of one state being under complete control by its counterpart. A number of scholars are critical of Myanmar-China relations, stating that Beijing is practising a form of "neo-colonisation"

---

[13]Poon Kim Shee, "The Political Economy of China-Myanmar Relations: Strategic and Economic Dimensions," op. cit., p. 48.

[14]Poon Kim Shee, "The Political Economy of China-Myanmar Relations: Strategic and Economic Dimensions," op. cit., p. 51.

of Myanmar amid the growing partnership. Others hinted that the large number of Chinese migrants to Myanmar is a potentially critical issue which might result in anti-Chinese riots similar to the one that broke out in 1967.[15] Some even argued that Myanmar is playing with fire in its close ties with China.[16] These views are but generalisations and it is necessary to give a more objective view of Myanmar-China relations.

Firstly, Myanmar-China relationship is mutually beneficial. China has been providing assistance to Myanmar in terms of technology and low-interest loan to help develop and industrialise Myanmar's domestic economy. The assistance covered a wide range of fields, from infrastructure development to improvement of the transportation system.[17] For instance, the Banglang Power Station, the largest hydro power station in Myanmar, was constructed with export credit of about US$250 million from China Export and Import Bank and completed in March 2005. It has a total installed capacity of 280,000 KW and annual output of 910 million kWh or nearly one third of the country's total demand for power. This power plant, to a great extent, eases the shortage in power supply in Myanmar.

Secondly, Myanmar has been gradually readjusting its China policy since 1988 accordingly to its evolving national interest. At the early stage of the military junta, Myanmar maintained close ties with China because it was not yet an ASEAN member country and its giant neighbour, India, together with the West was putting political and economic pressure on Myanmar. However, after the pressure eased and ASEAN advocated the "constructive engagement" policy from the early 1990s, the military junta began to decrease its dependency on China and advocated "equal-distance foreign policies" towards ASEAN, China and India.[18] After the 1997 Asian financial crisis, Myanmar continued

---

[15]Denny Roy, *China's Foreign Relations*, p. 174. Donald M. Seekins, "Burma-China Relations: Playing with Fire," *Asian Survey*, Vol. 37, No. 6, p. 530. Poon Kim Shee, "The Political Economy of China-Myanmar Relations: Strategic and Economic Dimensions," op. cit., p. 48.

[16]Donald M. Seekins, *Burma-China Relations: Playing with Fire*, op. cit., p. 539.

[17]Guo Kuan, Entering into Myanmar, Yunnan Fine Arts Press, 2004, pp. 25–29.

[18]Yue Deming, "A Preliminary Study of Myanmar's China Policy in the Post-Cold War Era," p. 58.

to adjust its foreign policy. Although it views China as an important partner, it continues to secure close ties with ASEAN and India. Myanmar's refusal to become a satellite state to China can also be seen in Myanmar's reluctance to reach an agreement on the China-Myanmar road-water project in 2001 after five years of negotiation and even when it is aware that the project is of strategic importance to Beijing.

Thirdly, there is no indication that Myanmar is giving China the most-favoured nation treatment and China is neither Myanmar's largest trade partner nor the biggest foreign investor of Myanmar. In fact, the military junta of Myanmar keeps closer and more frequent contact with the Thai government and it hosts visits by state heads and prime ministers of other Southeast Asian countries. Even the former Prime Minister Khin Nyunt, who was considered as a leader friendly to China, also kept close ties with government leaders of Singapore and Thailand. In military and security cooperation, the military junta is also in cooperation with other countries such as India and Russia.

Therefore, as stated by Shee Poon Kim, China-Myanmar entente is uneven, asymmetrical, but nevertheless reciprocal and mutually beneficial. The strategic partnership and economic relations are a marriage of convenience. Myanmar is neither a strategic pawn nor an economic pivot of China.[19] Tin Maung Maung Than also argues on the same ground noting that China-Myanmar relation should be evaluated under an appropriate environment, and that it is too simplified to describe Myanmar as a vassal state of China.[20]

3. China-Myanmar Relation and Myanmar's Democratisation

Myanmar's close economic relations with China were crucial to helping the country withstand the Western-led economic sanctions.[21] As Brad

---

[19]Shee Poon Kim, "The Political Economy of China-Myanmar Relations: Strategic and Economic Dimensions," op. cit., p. 34.

[20]Tin Maung Maung Than, "Myanmar and China: A Special Relationship?" *Southeast Asian Affairs 2003*, Singapore Institute of Southeast Asian Studies, pp. 189–210.

[21]Cai Yuming, "Breaking through the Two Ocean: A Study of China's Myanmar Policy," *Taiwan Journal of Humanity and Social Sciences in Fengjia*, No. 8, May 2004, p. 303.

Adams, Human Rights Watch's Director for Asia, stated in June 2005, the military junta survived international pressure because it has the backing of China, Thailand and India. He added that if China wants to be a leading nation it must stop providing economic and military assistance to the military junta.[22] Adams' comment is incorrect because China-Myanmar relations should not be viewed as a major obstacle to Myanmar's democratisation.

Firstly, the democratisation of Myanmar is a domestic issue. In terms of economic development, political culture and leadership, Myanmar is currently not ready to be a democratic entity. Comparatively, the military junta and other related groups under its control have absolute advantage over opposition parties and domestic ethnic minority groups. The latter is unlikely to be in a position to take over the military junta in the coming future.[23] The democratic movements in Myanmar (e.g. college students, monks and average citizens) not only did not show strong desire of overthrowing the military junta, they are more or less supportive of it.[24]

Secondly, China's national interest rather than Myanmar's domestic issues takes priority when it reinforces bilateral relations with the latter. Currently no domestic group is able to take over the military junta even if it is overthrown by an external power. Myanmar is most likely to be in chaos if the military junta loses control, bringing about uncertainty along the borders of China, India and Thailand. Both China and ASEAN are more concerned with Myanmar's stability rather than its problematic human rights record.[25]

Thirdly, China does pay attention to Myanmar's democracy and human rights issues in contrary to what is commonly believed to be.

---

[22]Xiao Jing, "Is China's Support on Rangoon an Obstacle to the International Sanction?" 12 June 2006, see http://www.voanews.com/chinese/archive/2005-06/w2005-06-11-voa23.cfm.

[23]Li Chenyang and Chen Yin, "Major Political Forces and Their Respective Impacts on Democratization in Myanmar," in *Contemporary Asia-Pacific*, No. 4, 2006, pp. 19–26.

[24]Kyaw Yin Hlaing, "Myanmar in 2004: Why Military Rule Continues," *Southeast Asian Affairs 2005*, Singapore Institute of Southeast Asian Studies, 2005, pp. 250–256.

[25]Xiao Jing, "Is China's Support on Rangoon an Obstacle to the International Sanction?" 12 June 2006, see http://www.voanews.com/chinese/archive/2005-06/w2005-06-11-voa23.cfm.

As Hu Jintao pointed out diplomatically during SPDC Vice President Maung Aye's visit in August 2003,

> As a friendly neighbour, China hopes that there will be national stability, harmony between ethnic groups, economic development, and happiness of people in Myanmar. China believes that the Myanmar's government will assess the situation properly and ensure that domestic situation will develop in a positive and constructive direction.[26]

China is a keen supporter of United Nations' (UN) mediation to bring about political dialogue between the ruling military junta and the National League for Democracy's Secretary-General Aung San Suu Kyi. China also endorses the ASEAN idea of "constructive intervention" or "comprehensive engagement" in Myanmar's domestic issues for possible political reform.[27] It is likely that China will continue to support ASEAN's resolution to help Myanmar develop peacefully and stably.[28]

4. Is China-Myanmar Military and Security Cooperation so Important?

Reports from the foreign media indicated that China had constructed deep-water seaports in Myanmar's southwest coastal islands and installed radars and electronic spying facilities. They also reported that Myanmar allowed China to use these facilities for the collection of intelligence or as naval bases for China's People's Liberation Army's Navy (PLAN).[29] The specific places mentioned in media reports are Coco Island, Hgyi island, Mergui, Thilawa Island, Zadetkyi Island, Kyaukpyu and Sittwe. The media reports also purported that China's

---

[26]"Hu Jintao met Myanmar's SPDC Vice President," Xinhuanet, 22 August 2003, see http://news.xinhuanet.com/newscenter/2003-08/22/content_1040486.htm.

[27]Poon Kim Shee, "The Political Economy of China-Myanmar Relations: Strategic and Economic Dimensions," op. cit., p. 38.

[28]Zou Keyuan, "China's Possible Role in Myanmar's National Reconciliation," *The Copenhagen Journal of Asian Studies* Vol. 17, 2003, p. 71.

[29]Poon Kim Shee, "The Political Economy of China-Myanmar Relations: Strategic and Economic Dimensions," op. cit., p. 36.

presence in the Indian Ocean will be a threat to ASEAN in the long run. It will also bring problems to the long-term strategic interest of India, Japan and the United States.[30]

These reports, however, did not reflect the real situation of China-Myanmar military and security cooperation. The strategic thinking of the military junta makes it clear that the above reports are inaccurate. Myanmar's military has no trust for any external power including China, because the Myanmar leaders are deeply nationalistic. The Myanmar leadership has been socialised under a political culture of distrust[31] and is fully aware of the potential danger of Myanmar becoming China's strategic pawn if they had maintained close military and security ties with China. To pre-empt such developments, it adopted a "Counter-Hedging Strategy" by reinforcing multilateral relations, especially with India, ASEAN and even Western countries. It also has increased military purchases from India, Russia and Pakistan to decrease its military dependence on China.

Deeply suspicious of any outside influence, it is unlikely that Myanmar would allow China's military agencies to set up bases within its territory. The presence of Chinese military agencies on these islands is to provide logistic and operational services to Myanmar's military rather than to build permanent PLA bases.

Prospects of China-Myanmar Relations

As to the prospects of China-Myanmar relations, Shee Poon Kim inducts three scenarios: the alarmist, the pessimistic and the guardedly optimistic. He also points out that the scenario that is most likely to evolve depends on the answers to the following questions: First, how long can the military junta hold on to power? Second, can the military survive in the 21st century? Third, how does Myanmar's membership in ASEAN affect its strategic relationship with China? Fourth, what will

---

[30]Poon Kim Shee, "The Political Economy of China-Myanmar Relations: Strategic and Economic Dimensions," op. cit., p. 36.
[31]Poon Kim Shee, "The Political Economy of China-Myanmar Relations: Strategic and Economic Dimensions," op. cit., p. 38.

be the attitude of the US, the EU, Japan and India towards Myanmar? Fifth, how far will Myanmar tilt towards China? The answer to this last question will also depend on the extent of the success or failure of Myanmar's economic development and its free market policy.[32]

Shee, however, missed out on the geopolitical factor. This paper will supplement this point in the following arguments:

1. The Military Junta is Unlikely to Change its Policy Towards China Due to a Number of Geopoliticial and Geoeconomical Factors

In geopolitics, the most important is the peripheral environment and the geographical distance among countries. The positive or negative impact or influence of one country on another is dependent on their distance.[33] In the case of China and Myanmar, the two countries share a common borderline of 2,200 kilometres with convenient access to each other's territory. Myanmar views China as not only a huge neighbour, but also a permanent member of the United Nations Security Council. As a result, Myanmar looks towards China for its support in dealing with issues that are most likely to draw international attention such as battling the armed ethnic minority groups in northern Myanmar. Since Myanmar is not and is unlikely to become a regional power in Southeast Asia, it does not need to depend on another great power to contain China. Furthermore, Myanmar is somewhat dependent on China economically. In particular, the economy of the upper northern part of Mandalay heavily relies on China. Myanmar will thus want to benefit from China's economic growth.

Although China has strong geopolitical and geoeconomical impact on Myanmar, it is evident that the Myanmar leadership does not have any intention to balance China's influence by aligning with the United States, India, Japan or other western countries. Like other members of ASEAN, Myanmar continues to adopt a foreign policy that aims

---

[32]Poon Kim Shee, "The Political Economy of China-Myanmar Relations: Strategic and Economic Dimensions," op. cit., pp. 48–49.

[33]Ye Zicheng, *Geopolitics and China's diplomacy*. Beijing Publishing House, 1998, p. 16.

to balance the influence of major powers. Even if there is a change in leadership, it is unlikely that Myanmar will alter its foreign policy.

2. China-Myanmar Relations Are Mutually Beneficial and Both Sides Will Continue to Expand Cooperation in other Fields

Beijing needs a stable and amicable external environment for its peaceful development. To this end, China will pursue neighbourliness as well as provide assistance whenever necessary. China's current and future policy towards Myanmar is and will aim to establish long-term economic and security cooperation regardless of the ideology of its government and as long as it does not become a strategic pawn of some other countries or organisations to contain China's development.

China will speed up economic cooperation with Myanmar in the fields of agriculture, human resources, natural resources and infrastructural construction. The two countries will also reinforce cooperation in bilateral trade, investment and energy development. Myanmar's geographical location also proves itself to be an important strategic option for Beijing to transport its energy supplies. Furthermore, the country's abundant oil reserve will enable it to play a role in China's oil imports.

Finally, as stated by Shee, despite growing Chinese influence, Myanmar will never become a strategic satellite state to China. Myanmar's strong sense of nationalism together with its past ability to successfully withstand foreign pressure and its determination to preserve its independence and cultural identity will most likely make Myanmar withstand preponderance of any external power.[34]

---

[34]Poon Kim Shee, "The Political Economy of China-Myanmar Relations: Strategic and Economic Dimensions," op. cit., pp. 18–19.

Vietnam-China Relations: Present and Future

Do Tien Sam

The geographical, economic and cultural landscape of Vietnam as well as the multi-faceted mutual influence and interactions between Vietnam and China have allowed Vietnam-China bilateral relations to occupy an important position in Beijing's foreign policy. This article describes and analyses the achievements and issues in Vietnam-China relations since the normalisation of bilateral relations in 1991, and provides several opinions on the prospect of relationship between both countries in the coming years.

Achievements and Issues in Bilateral Relations

1. Main Achievements

a) The Political and Diplomatic Aspect

Since the normalisation of bilateral relations in 1991, Vietnamese and Chinese State and Party leaders have been exchanging visits regularly. This has significantly contributed to enhancing mutual trust and understanding between the two sides and the comprehensive and steady development of bilateral relations. The exchanges have also helped to resolve many outstanding problems, including the border issue.[1]

---

[1]Vietnam-China Joint Communiqueù dated 10 November 1991 stated as follows: "Vietnam and China will develop the relationship of friendship and friendly neighbourhood on the basis of five principles: respect for each other's sovereignty and territorial integrity, non-aggression, non-intervention in each other's internal affairs, mutual beneficial equality and peaceful co-existence." "The Communist Party of Vietnam and the Communist Party of China will restore normal relations on the basis of the principles of independence, equality, mutual respect and non-interference in each other's internal affairs."

During the visits, leaders from both sides have signed seven Joint Communiqués (in 1991, 1992, 1994, 1995, 2004, 2005 and 2006) and seven Joint Declarations (in 1999, 2000, 2001 and 2006). At a summit meeting in February 1999, both sides agreed to strengthen Vietnam-China relations according to the principles of "friendly neighbourhood, comprehensive cooperation, durable stability and future-oriented outlook". Furthermore, the visits also saw the signing of many agreements aimed at strengthening and consolidating relations between ministries, especially by the foreign, security and defence services of both countries. The two countries also agreed to continue strengthening the mechanism for exchanging viewpoints on bilateral, regional and international issues of mutual concern and interest. Besides, the two countries have enhanced cooperation and collaboration at multilateral forums such as the UN, ARF, East Asia cooperation process, APEC and ASEM. In addition, exchanges between various sectors, mass organisations and localities of the two countries were also held every year. For instance, in recent years, youth organisations in Vietnam and China have carried out a number of youth exchange programmes.

It may be argued that bilateral political and diplomatic relations have never been as good as at present. Furthermore, the good political relations have created the momentum for further bilateral economic, cultural and other cooperation, and helped resolve effectively the outstanding issues left behind from the past, including the border issue.

b) *The Economic Aspect*

Propelled by normalised political and security relations since 1991 and aided by economic complementarity and favourable geographic conditions, Vietnam-China economic cooperation is also improving rapidly, especially in trade, investment and tourism. Bilateral trade increased by more than 200 fold from US$30 million in 1991 to US$8.2 billion in 2005. Specifically, the value of exports from Vietnam to China increased by over 220 fold from US$10 million in 1991 to US$2.55 billion in 2005, while exports from China to Vietnam increased by over 200 fold from US$20 million in 1991 to US$5.6 billion in 2005, exceeding the target of US$5 billion in 2005 previously put forward by the two countries' leaders.[2] In addition, China's foreign direct investment (FDI) in Vietnam has seen rapid growth in recent years. By August 2005, China's total FDI in Vietnam reached about US$710.4 million with 346 projects, making China the 14th largest FDI investor in Vietnam.[3]

Besides trade and investment, tourism between the two sides is also experiencing rapid growth. According to official statistics, Chinese tourist arrivals to Vietnam increased by more than 70 fold from 10,000 in 1991 to 778,431 in 2004, accounting for one third of Vietnam's total tourist arrivals.[4] In the first six months of 2005, Chinese arrivals were about 560,000, making them the largest in Vietnam.[5] At the same time, many Vietnamese have chosen China as their favourite tourist destination. In recent years, China registered about 20,000 Vietnamese tourist arrivals per year.

The Chinese government is also providing loans to Vietnam. In fact, it has offered a non-reimbursable grant of RMB200 million and a soft loan of about US$300 million to help the country improve its infrastructure and expand the production capacity of several important sectors.[6]

c) *The Cultural, Educational and Scientific Aspect*

Vietnam and China are also stepping up efforts to increase cooperation in cultural exchanges, education and science and technology. Since

---

[2]The trade statistics are calculated from the Statistics of China's Customs. However, according to the statistics of Vietnam's Customs, the two-way trade volume between Vietnam and China in 2005 reached US$8.7 billion, instead of US$8.2 billion. Tables 1 and 2 provide further annual information on bilateral trade as well as its breakdown in 2003.

[3]Hoang Lan, "Breakthroughs in Sino-Vietnamese Economic and Trade Relation," *Financial Times*, 28 April 2005. Tables 3 and 4 supply data on China's FDI by industries and by provinces in Vietnam.

[4]Nguyen Thi Thuy, *Sino-Vietnamese Relations: Events from July 2004–Jun 2005* (Institutional Projects), Hanoi: Institute of Chinese Studies, 2005, p. 4.

[5]Tourism Statistics, Vietnam's General Office of Tourism, posted at http://vietnamtourism.com/v–pages/news/index.asp.

[6]Information posted at http://vietnamnet.Vietnam/tinnoibat/2005/07/468911.

the normalisation of bilateral relations, cultural cooperation between the two countries have been developing rapidly. The two countries have signed various agreements, plans and programmes of cultural cooperation such as the Vietnam-China Agreement on Cultural Cooperation to further encourage more exchanges and cooperation in areas such as arts and literature, gymnastics and sports, press, audio and visual broadcasting, cinema, library, museum, art performance, exhibition and publications. Furthermore, Vietnam has sent hundreds of delegations to China for training and performance, and to participate in exhibitions. On the other hand, Chinese performers have staged numerous performances in Vietnam and received warm welcome from Vietnamese colleagues and public. The Chinese government also offered Vietnam RMB150 million to build the Vietnam-China Cultural Palace in Hanoi.

Table 1. Import-Export Volume of Vietnam and China (1991–2005) (mil. US$)

Year	Total		Vietnam's Exports		Vietnam's Imports	
	Value	Growth Rate %	Value	Growth Rate %	Value	Growth Rate %
1991	30		10		20	
1992	180	500	70	600	110	450
1993	400	122	120	71.4	280	155
1994	530	32.5	190	58.3	340	21.4
1995	1,050	98.1	330	73.6	720	111.7
1996	1,150	9.5	310	−0.7	840	16.6
1997	1,440	25.2	360	16.1	1,080	28.6
1998	1,245	−13.6	271	−39.2	1,028	−0.5
1999	1,318	5.8	354	63.1	964	−0.6
2000	2,466	87.1	929	62.4	1,537	59.4
2001	2,814	14.1	1,010	8.7	1,804	17.4
2002	3,223	14.5	1,340	32.6	1,883	4.3
2003	4,634	43.8	1,456	8.7	3,178	68.7
2004	7,190	55.1	2735	87.8	4,355	37.0
2005	8,200	14	2550	−6	5,650	30

Table 2. Structure of Imported-Exported Goods of China and Vietnam in 2003 (10,000 US$)

Items	China's Exports	Vietnam's Exports	Annual Growth Rate %	
			China's Exports	Vietnam's Exports
Volume	317852	145580	47.9	30.5
I. Goods for preliminary treatment	104470	119247	74.4	20.4
Fresh food	24646	13847	79.4	19.5
Vegetables	8933	11059	50.8	24.5
Coffee and tea	303	938	−8.5	48
Raw materials (excluding fuel)	5806	17752	26.6	44.1
Rubber	531	10428	−13.2	22.4
Wood	90	1064	38.4	54.2
Minerals and wasted metal materials	56	3930	130.3	119.8
Fuels and lubricating oils	72008	87275	80.3	16.5
Coals, coke coals and briquette	811	5375	85.9	5.9
Petroleum oils, refined	71196	81900	80.2	17.2
Aninal and Botanical Oils. wax	8	374	198.9	88.7
II. Manufactured goods	213382	26333	37.7	111.1
Chemical and finished products	51567	5073	78.1	54.6
Fertilisers (excluding group 272)	24524	1	260.5	0
Unprocessed plastic	1547	700	25.2	626.7
Materials and chemical products	5641	2944	21.7	105.2
Manufactured goods by materials	71746	9846	43.7	206.8
Leathers	3147	272	52	48.4
Rubber	1947	5744	30.7	661.4
Paper	1522	48	13.9	250.9
Textile fabrics	36348	2445	66.2	50.1
Iron and steel	12094	568	14.2	174.8
Coloured metal	3874	196	73.2	201.1
Metal products	6505	153	27.4	563.9
Machinery apparatus and parts or transportation	65186	7505	5.6	91.3
Diesel machines	10024	1117	−26.5	228.2
Machinery for industry	10925	129	15.2	60.9
Machinery for common industry	14063	2451	49.9	18.6
Machinery for power-generated industry	9438	2796	56.4	247.4
Manufactured products	24864	3909	73	89.6
Embroiders and costumes materials	12222	936	93.5	499.7
Footwear	3010	1846	43.7	130

Table 3. China's FDI in Vietnam by Industries (as at 22 August 2005; only active projects are included)

No	Industries	# Projects	Percentage	Total Invested Capital	Percentage
I	Industry	247	71%	423,834,452	60%
	Light Industry	65		99,335,452	
	Heavy Industry	136		238,367,917	
	Food Industry	20		23,573,718	
	Construction	26	16%	62,557,773	
II	Agriculture. forestry and Fishery	54		95,682,033	13%
	Agriculture and forestry	41		66,108,506	
	Fishery	13		29,537,527	
	Service	45	13%	190,960,869	27%
	Transport; storage and communications	7		7,360,000	
	Hotels, restaurants and travels	6		46,388,448	
	Financial intermediation	1		15,000,000	
III	Education and training	13		10,778,000	
	Real estate, renting business activities	3		40,000,000	13%
	EPZ and Industrial Zone Infrastructure Construction	1		55,500,000	
	Other services	13		15,934,421	
Total		346	100%	710,477,762	100%

Table 4. China's FDI by Provinces in Two China-Vietnam Economic Corridors (as at 31 December 2003) (US)

No	Province	# Projects	Total Capital	Registered Capital	Performed Capital
1	Hanoi	44	60,989,062	34,625,826	10,683,817
2	Hai Phong	23	53,525,520	23,545,520	18,824,521
3	Quang Ninh	19	42,894,878	17,578,290	8,418,222
4	Lao Cai	12	16,511,340	12,310,895	5,577,495
5	Lang Son	9	13,720,000	6,873,077	2,900,000
6	Ha Giang	2	5,925,000	2,633,000	
7	Lai Chau	1	1,500,000	1,500,000	

In education, the two countries have signed various agreements to increase cooperation and exchanges. One area of interest is to increase offers of scholarship from both sides. The total number of Vietnamese students who are granted scholarships to study in China per year is 130. In return, Vietnam offers 15 scholarships to Chinese students to study in Vietnam per year. By now, more than 30 universities in Vietnam have cooperation and exchanges with over 40 universities and institutes in China. Furthermore, there is an increasing number of self-supporting Vietnamese studying in China. According to official statistics, in 2004 alone, there were 4,382 Vietnamese students under long-term and short-term scholarships in China. This made Vietnamese the fourth largest group of students studying in China after the South Koreans, Japanese and Americans.[7]

Since 1991, Vietnam-China cooperation in science and technology has also been strengthened. The two countries have signed the Agreement and Protocol on Scientific and Technical Cooperation in which priority is given to cooperation in agricultural science and technology, especially in the processing of farm products and the building of high-tech farm production zones such as the project on

---

[7]China's Ministry of Foreign Affairs, *China's Diplomacy 2005*. Beijing: China's Ministry of Foreign Affairs, 2005, p. 505.

cross-bred rice and high-quality vegetables and fruits. The two countries have also implemented other projects such as the preservation and duplication of fruits that are on the verge of extinction, the study and management of the effective use of natural resources, water supply from the Mekong and Red Rivers, as well as cooperation in protecting the environment.

In the field of theoretic research, the two countries have successfully organised four major workshops, namely the "Socialism-Universality and Specificity" Workshop in Beijing in June 2000, the "Socialism-Vietnam's Experience and China's Experience" Workshop in Hanoi in November 2000, the "Socialism and Market Economy" Workshop in Beijing in October 2003, and the "Building the Ruling Party" Workshop in Hanoi in February 2004. With regards to cooperation in social and human sciences, the Vietnamese Academy of Social Sciences has signed cooperation agreements with the Chinese Academy of Social Sciences and other institutes of social sciences in Guangdong, Guangxi, Sichuan, Shanxi and Shanghai. These agreements have encouraged hundreds of researchers from both sides to undertake study tours, surveys and scientific exchanges. Furthermore, the Vietnamese Academy of Social Sciences in collaboration with the Guangxi Institute of Social Sciences have conducted joint research on Vietnam's economic renovation versus China's economic reform. The Vietnamese Academy of Social Sciences has also collaborated with the Shanghai Institute of Social Sciences in successfully organising the China-ASEAN Workshop in October 2004.

d) *Border and Territorial Issues between the Two Countries*

Resolving the border issue is one of the major achievements in Vietnam-China relations. The three areas of disputes have been important yet sensitive issues in the bilateral relations. These three areas are the land border, the Tonkin Gulf and the territorial claims in the Bien Dong Sea, including the Paracel Islands and the Spratly Islands. Therefore, right after the normalisation of bilateral relations in 1991, leaders from both sides have made substantial efforts to resolve the problem.

In the Joint Communiqué signed in November 1991, both countries affirmed that "they have agreed to resolve the existing border and territorial issues between the two countries through peaceful negotiations". In this spirit and with intensive efforts from both sides, on 30 December 1999, Vietnam and China concluded the Agreement on Land Border that took effect on 6 July 2000. On the basis of this Agreement, both countries aimed to resolve the delimitation and demarcation issues by 2008 and establish a border management instrument. This is an important achievement as it ensures peace and stability in the Vietnam-China border.

To solve the Tonkin Gulf demarcation problem, China and Vietnam concluded the Tonkin Gulf Demarcation Agreement and Agreement on Fisheries Cooperation in December 2000. After the agreement took effect in June 2004, both sides have been working together to maintain the security of the gulf and in the exploration and exploitation of the resources in the area. With this agreement both nations have effectively solved the second outstanding territorial issue and created favourable conditions for durable management and maintenance of stability in the Tonkin Gulf. This agreement also contributes to enhancing mutual trust and building momentum for the comprehensive development of cooperation between the two countries. Both China and Vietnam are now negotiating intensively on cooperation in the exploration and exploitation of oil and gas, joint survey on fishing resources in the joint fishing area in the Tonkin Gulf, joint patrol of the gulf, as well as the delimitation of the outer area of the Tonkin Gulf.

In parallel with peaceful negotiations to resolve the land border and Tonkin Gulf demarcation issues, the two countries have agreed to establish a working group on sea issues to promote dialogue and communications since 1993. In the Joint Declarations issued in 1999 and 2000, China and Vietnam pledged to:

> … continue to maintain the current mechanism of negotiations on sea issues, and persist in seeking a mutually accepted basic and durable solution through peaceful negotiations. Pending the final solution to the problem, both sides will actively discuss and look for possibilities of cooperation on sea in the areas of sea environmental protection, meteorology and hydrographs, and disaster management. Both sides agree to refrain from actions that can complicate or expand disputes, reasonably

resolve emerging issues in a constructive spirit, and prevent the difference on these issues from affecting the normal development of bilateral relations.

To avoid complications and to maintain the security of the Bien Dong Sea (South China Sea), both sides have agreed to abide by the principles provided in the "Declaration on the Conduct of Parties in the Bien Dong Sea", the common understanding of both countries' leaders as well as multilateral commitments. Especially, in March 2005, three oil companies from Vietnam, China and the Philippines signed the Agreement on Joint Conduct of Seismic Survey in the Bien Dong Sea.

In conclusion, the signing of the Agreement on Land Border, the Tonkin Gulf Demarcation Agreement and the Agreement on Fisheries Cooperation between Vietnam and China are the most important accomplishments in Vietnam-China bilateral relations. By solving the border issue, these agreements will help create new momentum for stronger cooperation in the coming years.

2. Existing Problems in Vietnam-China Relations

Although Vietnam-China relation has been improving rapidly, it is still facing a number of problems. Firstly, Vietnam's trade deficit is growing in its trade with China. From 2000 to June 2004, Vietnam's excessive imports stood at US$2.8 billion or 36 percent of Vietnam's total value of export to China.[8] This was aggravated by the ineffective handling of smuggling and trade rigging in border trade, causing numerous adverse socio-economic impacts on border localities. Furthermore, although China's FDI in Vietnam is increasing rapidly in both capital and portfolio, the quality of investment remains low. For example, the average investment capital per project is low, term of investment is short and equipment and technology is not advanced.

Secondly, both sides have yet to improve the expediency, facilities and infrastructure of several land border checkpoints. Immigration

---

[8]Hoai Son, "Trade Ties with China: Too Unbalanced," *Business Forum Newspaper*, Vol. 79, 6 October 2004, p. 4.

procedures and goods clearance as well as other formalities like quarantining and fee collection have yet to be streamlined. For instance, the transport systems such as roads, railways and waterways connection along the border areas have not been upgraded. Furthermore, there is also a shortage of direct airways between the major cities of the two countries. These deficiencies are hindering the increasing flow of people and goods between the two countries and undermining the advantage of the two country's geographic proximity.

Thirdly, despite taking steps to resolve the border issues, more work still need to be done to consolidate the results. Furthermore, both countries have yet to solve their territorial disputes in the Bien Dong Sea. Border issues are very sensitive issues and if they are not dealt with appropriately, they could easily undermine the burgeoning Vietnam-China relations.

Prospects of Vietnam-China Relations

1. *Favourable Factors Strengthening Bilateral Relations*

Despite some existing problems, Vietnam and China will most likely continue to strengthen and consolidate existing ties in the coming years. This is because of the following factors: First, Vietnam and China are neighbouring countries with long standing cultural and historic ties. Traditionally, the two countries share historical experience and have had long friendship in their struggle for national liberation and national building. These geographic, historical and cultural factors naturally bond their people together to create a mutually dependent and inseparable relationship.

Second, Vietnam and China have many similarities in their political, economic and social domains. Both countries are socialist oriented and under the leadership of a communist party. They are also implementing the open-door and renovation policy to industrialise their economy and modernise the country. Both sides are also learning from each other in this area by conducting numerous exchanges and consultation. Third, both countries want to maintain good relations with each other as well as their neighbours in order to create a peaceful and stable environment.

Such an environment would enable both nations to focus on economic development. For this reason, it is essential that both sides strictly abide by the signed agreements or treaties and "prevent the difference on these issues from affecting the normal development of bilateral relations" regarding existing border and territorial issues between the two countries, especially territorial dispute in the Bien Dong Sea.

2. Measures to Strengthen Vietnam-China Relations

First of all, both sides should be fully aware that the long-standing friendship between the Vietnamese and the Chinese people is invaluable and should be preserved. Second, relevant sectors and authorities in China and Vietnam should also build on the numerous agreements and declarations stated in their joint communiqués and joint declarations. They can find ways to advance cooperation in a practical and effective manner. For example, economic researchers of the two countries should conduct joint studies on measures to realise the idea of "two corridors, one economic belt". They can figure out a way to connect these three areas with the East-West Corridor and the Trans-Asia route. By doing so, they can take advantage of Vietnam's position as the link to the two provinces of Guangxi and Yunnan in China in the future ASEAN-China Free Trade Area. They can also utilise Vietnam's position as the bridge to China's eastern coastal provinces in the East Asia cooperation process, thereby "lifting" the two economies in transition.

Finally, on cooperation in social and human sciences, both sides should thoroughly review the achievements as well as shortcomings, and then select the topics or issues of mutual concern for joint study, comparison or seminars among their universities or research centres. This is to identify the experience of universality for mutual consultation and exchange.

Settling Problems and Looking Ahead

Since the normalisation of bilateral relations in 1991, Vietnam-China relations have undergone rapid development and have made many important achievements in the political, economical and cultural fields.

Both sides have also settled many outstanding problems, most notably, the border and territorial issues.

At a time when the world and the Asia-Pacific region are witnessing complicated and unpredictable developments, China and Vietnam are consolidating and enhancing their relations. The rapid progress in Vietnam-China relations not only meets the durable and fundamental interest of both countries but is also bringing peace, cooperation and development to the region.

References

1. Vietnam-China Joint Declarations in 1999, 2000, 2001, 2005, and 2006.
2. Vietnam-China Joint Communiqueùs in 1991, 1992, 1994, 1995, 2004, 2005 and 2006.
3. Do Tien Sam-Furuta Motoo (ed), *The Vietnam's "Multilateralization and Diversification" Foreign Policy and Sino-Vietnamese Relations*. Hanoi: Social Sciences Publisher, 2003.
4. Nguyen Minh Hang (ed), *China-Vietnam's Border Trade: History, Present, and Prospect*. Hanoi: Social Sciences Publisher, 2001.
5. Center for Chinese Studies (Vietnam), *China-Vietnam's Economic and Cultural Relations: Present and Prospect*. Hanoi: Social Sciences Publisher, 2001.
6. Dai Kelai (ed), *The Prospect for Sino-Vietnam Relations in the 21st Century*. Hongkong Press for Social Sciences Ltd., 2003.
7. He Shengda (ed), *The Construction of the ASEAN-China Free Trade Area and Yunnan's Opening to Southeast Asia*. China: Yunnan People's Publisher. 2003.
8. *Chinese Studies Review* (Vietnam) issues in 2004 and 2005.
9. Vietnam's Ministry of Trade, http://www.mot.gov.vn
10. Vietnam's Ministry of Planning and Investment, http://www.mpi.gov.vn
11. Vietnam's National Administration of Tourism, http://www.Vietnamtourism.com
12. General Department of Vietnam Customs, http://www.customs.gov.vn

ASEAN-China Relations:
Indonesia's Perspective

Ignatius Wibowo Wibisono

In comparison to other ASEAN countries, Indonesia has the most turbulent relationship with China. It began with a very positive start by Indonesia when, in 1950, it recognised the independence of the People's Republic of China (PRC). Indonesia was among the first of a handful countries to recognise China, although it was the Republic of China (ROC), the predecessor to the PRC in mainland China until 1949, which recognised Indonesia's independence in 1945 (The nationalists who led the ROC fled to Taiwan after 1949, declared the government as the ROC, and competed against the PRC for international recognition). Indonesia-China relations went well until about the middle of the 1950s when the problem of dual citizenship emerged. The relationship did not improve even after the problem was settled; in fact, it worsened in 1967 when the two countries severed diplomatic relations.

The year 1967 was marked by another important event, the establishment of ASEAN. On the initiative of President Suharto at that time, ASEAN was set up to counter China which was very aggressive in sponsoring "revolutionary movements" across Southeast Asia. ASEAN, indeed, was perceived as the creation of the United States of America. Understandably, in the heat of the Cold War, China was in no mood to reconcile with ASEAN, not the least Indonesia.

Indonesia and China, therefore, have a complex relationship in which history plays an important role. It is the low ebb of history that matters most. The author's argument is that although China has changed, there is still a perception of the unchanging China in some groups of people in Indonesia. There are two groups of people under consideration: the bureaucrats and the academics. Each in its own way remains highly suspicious of China.

The Bureaucrats

Bureaucrats are well known for their resilience to change. This is also true for bureaucrats who are, in one way or another, involved in foreign affairs such as the Department of Foreign Affairs, Department of Internal Affairs, the bureau of intelligence, and the embassies.

There is, certainly, among bureaucrats a view that China is rising and rising fast. This view is reflected in a publication by the Department of Foreign Affairs, *AKSES*.[1] The titles of the articles are *"Gaya Hidup dan Peluang Dagang"*[2] and *"Jejak Geliat Sang Naga."*[3] The authors acknowledge with much admiration that the economic development of China is spectacular. The first article states that *"sejak menganut ekonomi terbuka, pertumbuhan ekonomi China melesat mencapai angka rata-rata 9 percent per tahun"*,[4] while the second one agrees that *"Tidak bisa dimungkiri saat ini China merupakan salah satu raksasa ekonomi dunia."*[5]

But there is also a note of caution. The following three articles of the same edition have the following titles: *"Mengejar Hoki di Negeri Feng Shui,"*[6] *"Tak Mudah Cari Untung di China,"*[7] *"Awas, Banjir, Banjir."*[8] The first and second articles basically argue that it is difficult for Indonesia to sell their products to China because the Chinese prefer products from the West. They agree that though the Chinese have opened up their market to the world after WTO accession, Chinese exports to Indonesia have been so overwhelming that Indonesia's market is simply flooded by

---

[1] *Akses*, Vol. 2 (August 2006)
[2] "Life Style and Trade Opportunity," Ibid., p. 6.
[3] "The Trace of the Waking Dragon," Ibid., p. 7–8.
[4] Translated: "Since the beginning of the opening up, the Chinese economy has grown rapidly at 9 percent per year."
[5] Translated: "It is undeniable that China has transformed herself into an economic giant."
[6] "To Grab 'Hoki" in Fengshui Country," Ibid., p. 9–10.
[7] "Not Easy To Get Profit in China," Ibid., p. 11–13.
[8] "Be Careful, A Big Flood Is Coming," Ibid., p. 14–15.

Chinese goods. *"Merebaknya industri China itu tentu saja menyebabkan negara-negara yang basis industrinya masih redup praktis terbanjiri produk 'negeri tirai bambu' tersebut."*[9] The articles, then, quote a series of statistics which show the sharp increase in Chinese products entering the Indonesian market, and the collapse of Indonesian enterprises which were unable to compete with Chinese products.

These articles display an ambiguous reaction of both admiration and fear. The same sentiment is prevalent among bureaucrats at the Department of Internal Affairs. In a seminar organised by the Department of Foreign Affairs in Jakarta on 7 December 2006,[10] the Department of Internal Affairs representative presented a list of "obstacles to the relations with China"[11] (see Table 1).

Table 1. Potential Problems Arising from the RI-PRC Relations

1.	Relations with Taiwan
2.	Existence of Falun Gong organisation in Indonesia
3.	Visit of Dalai Lama to Indonesia
4.	Emergence of laws by local government that are unfavourable to business
5.	Citizenship problem in the marriage between Indonesian citizens and Chinese citizens
6.	The demand by the Chinese Embassy in Jakarta for its former assets
7.	The smuggling of Chinese products into Indonesia, especially electronics and garments
8.	Unfair trade practice (dumping) by China in the international markets
9.	Illegal logging and illegal fishing which find markets in China
10.	Chinese citizens involved in the drug trafficking and drug production in Indonesia

Source: Agung Mulyana, Ibid., p. 2–3.

---

[9]Translated: "Countries with weak industrial basis felt flooded by products from the Bamboo Curtain."

[10]Roundtable Discussion Kemitraan Strategis RI-RRC, Tindak Lanjut Konkrit dan Prospek ke Depan, Jakarta, 7–8 Desember 2006.

[11]Agung Mulyana, *"Antisipasi Jajaran Departemen Dalam Negeri dan Pemda Terhadap Masalah Yang Timbul dalam Hubungan Bilateral RI-RRC"* [The Department of Internal Affairs and the Local Government Anticipate Problems Arising from the Bilateral Relations of Indonesia and China.]

Two issues could obstruct Indonesia-China relations. The recent visit of Taiwan President Chen Shuibian to Batam Island was cited. The possibility of the visit of Dalai Lama is also anticipated because of his visits to countries in the West. The issue of Falun Gong is in the grey area because Indonesia law allows the setting up of organisations. The Chinese embassy was reported to have asked the Jakarta Police to stop Falun Gong activities, something which is controversial in the light of state sovereignty.

Another grey area is the demand by the Chinese Embassy in Jakarta for their former assets (buildings) in Jakarta. According to the Jakarta Mayor Office, the Embassy has been very active and aggressive in pursuing its goal. They approached many persons at many levels of the mayor office, sending lawyers to demand for the return of the assets. In the process, the office received a kind of threat from the staff of the Embassy that this case could jeopardise Indonesia-China relations. It is doubtful that there is such a threat, however. The fact that such high emotions were displayed by Chinese diplomats suggests that something was amiss.

The rest of the issues are actually internal problems of Indonesia. Smuggling, for instance, is less a case of international relations than a case of the weakness of the Indonesian bureaucracy in preventing smuggling. This is also true for illegal logging and illegal fishing, and the operation of Chinese drug dealers in Indonesia. The speaker insists that this is a problem which China should solve. He forgets that it is the rampant corruption in Indonesia which makes these possible and it is up to the Indonesian government (police) to tackle the problems.

A lady from PPATK (Pusat Pelaporan dan Analisa Transaski Keuangan, an institution which deals with money laundering) added that China has a tendency to debilitate the system of a country if the country is weak. The US is a strong country which China finds difficulty to disrupt. This is not the case with Indonesia. Knowing that Indonesia is a weak country, she argues, China deliberately incapacitates the law-enforcement system of Indonesia. This assessment surprised the audience.

This spectrum of views reflects the bureaucrats' negative perception of China, attributable to the successful indoctrination of the era of

"Orde Baru" which sees China as a threat. "Orde Baru" took place only eight years ago and "Reformasi" in Indonesia has not reformed the bureaucracy. They still occupy their position, holding the old ideology. The Department of Internal Affairs is no exception in this case.

The most complex issue is related to "overseas Chinese". The bureau of intelligence is paying close attention to this group because of their potential threat to Indonesia security. At the Q&A session, one question put forward by the staff is about how some China-based ethnic organisations invited staff from Chinese embassies to their meetings. It implies that "overseas Chinese" are still connected to their homeland and maintain their loyalty to China, not to Indonesia. As China is growing in wealth, it is feared — so goes the argument — that this group of people will pose a threat to Indonesia.

It has to be noted that the person used the term "overseas Chinese" to refer to Indonesians of Chinese descent. It is not known whether the term was used out of ignorance. Giving him the benefit of the doubt, the use of the term "overseas Chinese" still reflects a deep suspicion of Indonesians of Chinese descent. They are Chinese who are living overseas, or in other words, they are not truly Indonesians. It seems that in the mind of these people a Chinese cannot become a citizen of a new country. There is another person who used the term "*huaqiao*" to refer to the same group, and used it without a clear distinction.

The Indonesian Embassy in Beijing is, perhaps, the only branch of government bureaucracy which actively promotes good relations with China. The current Ambassador, Sudrajat, speaks highly of China and encourages Indonesians to go to China and to take advantage of the openness of China. In fact, he has gone so far as to become a good PR for China. In the magazine *AKSES*, he criticised Indonesia for not being aggressive enough. "*Dibandingkan dengan negara ASEAN lain, Indonesia dirasa kurang agresif. Bagaimana tidak, Indonesia hanya memiliki satu konsulat jendral di China, yaitu di Guangzhou.*"[12]

In sum, except for the Indonesian Embassy in Beijing, bureaucrats in Indonesia are generally adopting an ambivalent attitude towards

---

[12]Sudradjat, "*Menanam Dolar di Ladang Bambu*" [To Plant Dollars in the Bamboo Field] *Akses*, Vol. 2 (August 2006), p. 18.

China. They do recognise China's power, especially its economic power. At the same time, they still harbour fear that this power will do harm to Indonesia. Dino Patti Djalal, in his presentation in the first session, cautioned the danger of *"xenophobia"*. Indonesian people, he said, cannot afford to harbour this phobia, including in their dealings with the Chinese.

The Academics

A series of seminars on Indonesia-China relations were organised by Centre for Strategic and International Studies (CSIS), Jakarta and by the Department of Foreign Affairs. The CSIS seminar was co-sponsored by the Chinese Embassy in Jakarta and presented by Chinese and Indonesisan speakers.[13] The speaker from CSIS, Eddy Prasetyono, reminded the audience that there are areas where potential conflict can erupt any time soon, such as the Straits of Malacca. All major powers are concerned about the safety of their oil vessels passing through the Straits from the Middle East. China is one of them. He argues that China is worried about the dominance of the American and Japanese in the Straits. China is therefore keen to preempt such moves by closing its ranks with ASEAN.

Another presenter, Natalia Soebagjo from the Centre for Chinese Studies showed how China has opened itself to the world but Indonesia is slow to respond. In her opinion the problem lies in the lack of trust between the two countries. The Indonesians are unable to get rid of the burden of the past, always seeing the Chinese, including the Chinese born in Indonesia, as a threat. Likewise, the Chinese in Mainland China could not forget the May Riots of 1998 in which the Chinese in Indonesia were brutally victimised. She concludes her paper by saying: "China's openness and the twenty years of increased people-to-people contact between Indonesia and China seem to have lessened Indonesia's suspicion of China, but the fear remains."[14]

---

[13]Seminar, "Sino-Indonesian Relations: Substantiating the Strategic Partnership between Indonesia and China," Jakarta, 9 May 2006.

[14]Natalia Soebagjo, "Sino-Indonesian Relations : Socio-Cultural Dimensions," Jakarta, May 2006.

In the "Roundtable Discussion" mentioned earlier, Indonesian Foreign Minister, Hasan Wirayuda, in his opening remark, pointed out that Indonesia had to respond to the rise of China. One and a half years after the signing of the "Strategic Partnership", there has been no action; he urged the participants to produce a concrete plan of action at the end of the seminar. The remark shows that Indonesia does not seem to be too enthusiastic about the partnership.

A number of reasons accounted for this. The first speaker, Brigadier General, Marsiano Norman from the Department of Defence, observes that China's defence budget has increased and it is building a blue-ocean navy which can be deployed as far as Southeast Asia. In addition to that, China is world number four country for exporting weapons across the globe. Mr Norman agrees that Indonesia can buy weapons from China but warns that this close relationship will have implication for Indonesia-America relations. Indonesia should not be too close to China at the expense of Indonesia-America relations, he said.

Kusnanto Anggoro, an observer of defence and military affairs from the CSIS, argues that Indonesia does not have a coherent defence policy with the consequence that China does not take Indonesia seriously. Kusnanto was talking about the military co-operation between Indonesia and China. It would be difficult for China to reciprocate to Indonesia's passivity. This is especially true with regard to non-traditional security issues which Indonesia is not well-prepared. But Kusnanto also points out that China would only sell the most advanced weapons to Pakistan.

The next speaker, C.P. Luhulima, explains the reluctance of Indonesia and ASEAN. In his view, ASEAN countries are not sure whether China will continue to be friendly. Rhetorically, he asked: "Will China become a 'big brother' to ASEAN countries?" This nagging question lingers among the elite who sees China as aggressive. That is why ASEAN countries develop a "hedging strategy" by approaching the United States, Japan and India. The Treaty of Amity and Cooperation between China and ASEAN (2003), in this perspective, is highly important in preventing China from achieving its goals. In similar vein, Indonesia must also demand that China abide by the Code of Conduct in the South China Sea (2002), and the Tractate of ASEAN as Free Nuclear Zone.

During the Questions & Answers session, almost all responses raised the issue of whether China could become a security threat to Indonesia. Eddy Prasetyono maintains that by the 2015–2020 period, when China needs more oil and its ships have to pass through Indonesia, there is a danger that China will use its military power to protect its interests. By that time China may swagger in Southeast Asia to exert its power. This line of argument is supported by Luhulima who again asked a penetrating question: "Why do you see China as if China is an angel?" Obviously, he was referring to the previous speakers who lavishly praised China for all its achievements. He strongly reminded the audience to be prepared when China changes its colour.

It is apparent that there are reservations among academics about China's rise. To some, China is posing a threat both militarily and economically. To others, though China is not a threat now, they are not sure it will remain so if China makes further progress in its development. Indonesia at the moment, interestingly, is not prepared to respond to China's rise adequately. It is to be noted that this view is not limited to academics who attended the "Roundtable" seminar.

Developing Soft Power

Bureaucrats and academics are two different groups with different agenda. Bureaucrats tend to be conservative, close-minded, whereas academics are said to have an inquisitive mind. Bureaucrats are empowered to implement policies while the academics have control over discourse in the society. The two normally do not see eye to eye. In this study, however, there is a convergence of views. Both acknowledge China's newly acquired power, and at the same time they share the view that China can pose a danger either at present or in the future.

This view is totally different from that of the government. In the past eight years, the Indonesian government has adopted a positive approach to China as testified by the visits of the President and Vice President to China. On each visit they signed Memoranda of Understanding on various issues, most of them economic. The Indonesian government had also, as part of ASEAN, agreed, in 2003, to sign the "Treaty of Amity and Cooperation" with China.

The difference in perception between bureaucrats and the Indonesian government may partly explain the slow implementation of the agreement on strategic partnership signed in April 2005. The implementation of the government's policy rests with the bureaucrats.

The Chinese government certainly has done its best to project a friendly China. If it wants to allay fear in Indonesia, China should develop its soft power to the fullest[15]. To the bureaucrats and academics, and indeed to the ordinary people in Indonesia, China still has to prove its soft power. In the author's view there is much to be done in this area if China wants to be accepted in Indonesia and ASEAN in general.

---

[15]Ignatius Wibowo, "*Berhadapan dengan Kekuatan Lunak (Soft Power) Cina*," [To Face the Soft Power of China] paper presented at the Roundtable Discussion Kemitraan Strategis RI-RRC, Tindak Lanjut Konkrit dan Prospek ke Depan, Jakarta, 7–8 Desember 2006.

China's Rise and Partnership with ASEAN

Wang Yan

China's economy has been growing at a remarkable speed for nearly three decades. Since it began restructuring its economy in 1978, the country's Gross Domestic Product (GDP) has increased more than tenfold. Furthermore, the living standard of the Chinese people has improved greatly. Little could one imagine that merely 25 years ago, the Chinese people had to use coupons to buy rice, oil and other basic necessities. But today, China's economy in purchasing power parity (PPP) terms is the second largest in the world after the United States.

However, China's rise has attracted a lot of attention. A country with a population of 1.3 billion has made history with its unprecedented growth rate, and the debate is not on its ability to rise, but on the direction of its rise. Located in a strategically important region with diverse states and cultures, China's rise is a concern for major powers which are in the Asia Pacific for multiple strategic interests: Is China's rise a peaceful one or a threat to the region?

Understanding the Impact of China's Economic Growth

To quell such fears, during the decades of development, the Chinese government has repeatedly stated that China has no intention of challenging the international system and stressed the importance of being a responsible member in the international community. Furthermore, it has recently put forward new concepts for its foreign policy orientation. The "New Security Concept", for instance, em- phasises on mutual and cooperative security, while the concept of "peaceful development" focuses on the commitment to non-violence.

Other concepts include the adoption of "win-win" cooperation and the building of a harmonious world. These concepts aim to refute the idea that Beijing is playing a zero-sum game in its foreign policy, promote unity and diversity, and use dialogue to solve conflicts. By incorporating these concepts in its foreign policy, Beijing wants to show that China has no intention of becoming a revolutionary state in the international system but to become a responsible member and a constructive partner in world affairs.

In addition, China's economic rise should not be viewed as an individual case. In other parts of the world, there are many countries experiencing strong economic growth. For instance, in Asia, ASEAN economies such as Vietnam together with India are growing. This trend can also be seen in Latin American countries such as Brazil, Mexico and Chile and the African states of South Africa, Nigeria and Egypt. Put together, these countries with a combined population of about 3.3 billion people have been enjoying substantial economic growth. This itself has created history, contributing significantly to world peace and development.

Furthermore, if China's economic rise is viewed in a larger context, China's rise is still at her initial stage and China remains an underdeveloped nation. China's per capita GDP still ranks below 100th in the world, and the gap between China's national capabilities and other major powers in the world especially the United States and Japan is quite wide. There is still a long way before China can catch up with these powers. In fact, it would take another 30 years before China could catch up with the United States in terms of GDP if the present growth rate is maintained. Moreover, China has many domestic problems to heed to. It is likely that within the coming 50 years China will concentrate on its domestic affairs, leaving little resources to pose a threat to others.

Finally, in a globalised and interdependent economy, China is sharing the benefits of her growth with Asia and other parts of the world. A study shows that in the last 10 years, the American manufacturing industry saved more than US$600 billon thanks to Chinese imports. This is the same with the European and the Japanese manufacturing industries. ASEAN countries also enjoyed this positive development. In fact, total bilateral trade between China and ASEAN increased from US$800 million in 1978 to US$105 billion in 2005, with ASEAN registering a trade surplus of US$20 billion. China's rise thus should not be viewed as a threat but an opportunity.

Assessing China-ASEAN Relations

For the past 15 years, China's engagement with ASEAN has been both positive and active. It has also shown its willingness to engage in multilateral dialogue with countries over regional disputes. From the Chinese perspective, ASEAN countries have individually or collectively helped China to realise its vision of creating a mutually beneficial multipolar order in the region. On the other hand, ASEAN countries accept China's interests in this region. This constructive relation is also helped by the Chinese leadership's awareness that China's rise has caused great concern among its neighbours and in the international community. To dispel concerns of a "China threat," China has adopted a policy of building good neighbourly relationships and forging partnerships with neighbouring countries.

This awareness is reflected in China's initiatives in participating in multilateral regional schemes. China actively participates in ASEAN-led regional institutions, such as the ASEAN Regional Forum (ARF) and ASEAN Plus one and plus three dialogues. China and ASEAN concluded the Joint Declaration of ASEAN and China on Cooperation in Field of Non-Traditional Security Issues and the Declaration on the Conduct of Parties in the South China Sea (DOC) in 2002. China was the first dialogue partner to accede to the Treaty of Amity and Cooperation (TAC) in Southeast Asia in 2003 which is an important gesture towards its acceptance of ASEAN norms. In the same year, China and ASEAN signed a Joint Declaration on Strategic Partnership for Peace and Prosperity. While the signing of the DOC showed the desire of both ASEAN and China to promote trust, confidence and cooperation and to accept a code of conduct in the disputed area, the accession by China to the TAC provided further reassurance to the peace and security of the region.

Consequently, with Beijing's friendly gestures, ASEAN countries began to accept China's rise as a reality. Now most countries in the region do not believe that a strong China will pose a security threat to them. Instead, many of them view China's participation as a critical component of the solution to some very important issues. Past and current developments have proved that China's rapid growth is not a competing force in the region. Rather, it has served as an impetus for greater growth. Many ASEAN leaders believe that the region suffered when China was weak and divided, and vice versa when China is growing and confident.

Consolidating Ties with ASEAN

There is great potential for future growth in China-ASEAN relations. In the past 16 years, both sides have enjoyed good political relations and rapid progress in economic cooperation. Leaders from China and ASEAN have continuously identified, developed and built on each other's common interests to create more channels for future cooperation. Under these active and positive interactions, China and ASEAN have strengthened consultation and coordination on regional and international issues. The two sides are working together to promote healthy institutional cooperation, such as ASEAN dialogues, ARF, Asia Cooperation dialogue, APEC and other regional cooperation mechanisms. Besides, the interactive mechanisms between China and ASEAN have been functioning effectively. China has also been supporting ASEAN's vision of more regional integration process, and the furthering of China-ASEAN partnership has contributed to the deepening of the process. Moreover, both ASEAN and China support open regionalism and welcome contributions from outside for peace, stability and prosperity of this region.

Undoubtedly, leaders from China and ASEAN are aware of the potential risks that the region faces. One example was the 1997 Asian financial crisis. Although it was a devastating challenge, it turned out to be a motivating force for more substantive cooperation. However, observers have pointed out that the incentives and cohesion created by the financial crisis is starting to show signs of weakening. Therefore, it is necessary for China and ASEAN to continue to work together to identify these problems and take immediate yet far-sighted actions.

One of the major issues over which China and ASEAN can further their partnership is cooperation in traditional and non-traditional security, which lags behind in comparison with economy and trade. Therefore, both sides should strengthen dialogue mechanisms in this area through more information exchanges to reduce uncertainty and remove suspicion and improve mutual trust.

The Future of China-ASEAN Partnership

ASEAN views China as a key player in the Asia-Pacific region and attached great importance to its relationship with China. The relationship between China and ASEAN should be considered in the broader strategic context of the Asia-Pacific region in which there are other stakeholders who have contributed and can continue to contribute to regional peace, stability and prosperity.

This is important especially to China which is at an important stage of its modernisation drive. It is pressing ahead with economic reform and opening up, which are beneficial to the region. Just as China's development is closely linked with ASEAN's prosperity, ASEAN is an important regional partner for China. It is thus imperative that ASEAN and China continue to build a strong foundation of mutual interests, based on economic cooperation and political solidarity. This is to allow both sides to harness their strengths to enhance the region's overall economic attractiveness and competitiveness.

Sixteen years' exploration and efforts have brought China-ASEAN relations to this level. Both sides have established a fruitful partnership, which has contributed to the peace and stability as well as the prosperity of the region. Relations have gone from strength to strength. However cooperation has yet to reach a new level of strategic partnership. It may well take the hard work and wisdom of several generations to realise the final goal of East Asia integration. But as long as these efforts to participate and contribute to this process are continued, this historical goal can be materialised.

92-97

ASEAN-China Relations and Development of East Asian Regionalism

Zhang Zhenjiang

Since the establishment of the ASEAN-China dialogue in 1991, ASEAN-China relations have been improving rapidly. The comprehensive and in-depth growth of bilateral relations between ASEAN and China is beneficial to both China and ASEAN member countries. Instead of focussing on an ASEAN or China experience, this paper studies the burgeoning ASEAN-China relations from an East Asian perspective. It argues that ASEAN-China bilateral relations are becoming the foundation and new engine for the sustainable development of East Asian regionalism. It also shows that ASEAN-China bilateral relations have far-reaching regional and global significance.

Rise of East Asia Regionalism

The rise of East Asia regionalism along with the rapid development of ASEAN-China relations is an important and unprecedented development. The idea of an East Asian community came from former Malaysian Prime Minister Dr. Mahathir Bin Mohamad when he proposed the formation of the East Asian Economic Grouping (EAEG) in 1990. Although Mahathir's plan failed to materialise, the idea of forming an East Asian community led to the establishment of other regional framework such as the Asia Pacific Economic Community (APEC) and, most importantly, the ASEAN plus Three (APT) process.

The APT is made up of China, Japan, Korea and ten ASEAN members — Indonesia, Malaysia, Singapore, Thailand, Philippines,

Cambodia, Laos, Myanmar, Brunei and Vietnam. The first informal APT summit took place at the height of the 1997 Asian financial crisis. The two events were not coincidental, but a relationship of cause and effect.[1] Furthermore, the APT summit was held just a year after China became a full dialogue partner in 1996. However, the APT did not make much progress in its first few years except with the annual summit declarations including the 1999 Joint Statement on East Asia Cooperation and a regional currency swap arrangement in 2000 known as the Chiang Mai Initiative. Nonetheless, there is great potential that the APT process could eventually lead to the creation of an East Asian community. This is clearly illustrated by the declaration of the China-ASEAN Free Trade Agreement (CAFTA) in 2001.

The CAFTA is the product of the ASEAN-China partnership or ASEAN plus One (China) process. It was declared in 2001 with the aim of establishing an ASEAN-China free trade zone by 2015. In 2002, China and ASEAN signed the Framework Agreement on Comprehensive Economic Cooperation. In 2003, the Protocol to Amend the Framework Agreement was signed and the "Early Harvest" programme was launched. In 2004, both sides reached the Agreement on Trade in Goods of the Framework Agreement and the tariff cut process started from 2005. The liberalisation of trade greatly benefitted ASEAN-China bilateral trade. For instance, China-ASEAN total trade volume jumped from US$78.25 billion in 2003 to US$130.37 billion in 2005. Total volume is anticipated to reach US$200 billion by 2010. The beneficial economic relations also encouraged China and ASEAN to strengthen cooperation in other fields such as security, politics and social exchanges.

The CAFTA and the rapid growth of China-ASEAN relations constitute a major part of East Asian regionalism and cooperation

---

[1]Richard Stubbs, "ASEAN Plus Three: Emerging East Asian Regionalism?," *Asian Survey*, Vol. 42, No. 3 (May/June 2002), pp. 440–55; Douglas Webber, "Two Funerals and a Wedding? The Ups and Downs of Regionalism in East Asia and Asia-Pacific after the Asian Crisis," *The Pacific Review*, Vol. 14, No. 3 (2001), pp. 339–72; Kevin G. Cai, "The ASEAN-China Free Trade Agreement and East Asian Regional Grouping," *Contemporary Southeast Asia*, Vol. 25, No. 3 (2003).

as it involved 1.8 billion people. It is also an initial step towards the realisation of an East Asian community, an idea that was shelved after Mahathir's failed attempt to create the EAEG in 1990. As a result, it can be argued that the real development of East Asian regionalism started from China-ASEAN relations.

At the same time, the success of China-ASEAN relations is exerting strong pressure on Japan and South Korea to strengthen their relations with ASEAN. The two countries, especially Japan, were reluctant to have institutionalised regionalism with ASEAN even though both sides enjoy strong economic relations. However, the deepening of cooperation between China and ASEAN changed the whole landscape in the region and prompted Japan and South Korea to initiate similar level of cooperation.

For instance, Japan signed the Framework for Comprehensive Economic Partnership with ASEAN in 2003 and joined the Treaty of Amity and Cooperation (TAC) in Southeast Asia in 2004. Tokyo also upgraded its relationship with ASEAN from "cooperative partnership" to "strategic partnership" in 2005. Similarly, South Korea joined TAC in 2004 and signed the Framework Agreement on Comprehensive Economic Cooperation with ASEAN in 2005. As for establishing an East Asian community, both Japan and South Korea are becoming more active in promoting the idea. Different initiatives have been proposed such as the East Asian Community by Japan, East Asian FTA and the Northeast Asian FTA.

The most significant development is the initiation of the East Asian Summit. The inaugural East Asian Summit was held in Kuala Lumpur in 2005, involving all APT countries and other regional countries — Australia, New Zealand and India. The inclusive nature of the summit shows that the effects of East Asian regionalism stimulated by ASEAN-China relations have already spilled over to a wider geographical region as non East Asian countries are joining the process of regional cooperation in East Asia. This is also important because these overlapping and sub-regional efforts will eventually contribute to the cooperation of the entire East Asia.

Concluding Remarks

Scholars and politicians in East Asia countries are having great expectations of various regional efforts in East Asia. Ideas and schemes like East Asian Community, East Asian No-War Community, East Asian Free Trade Area are being explored and discussed. Among them, three sets of bilateral relations cantered on ASEAN are developing competitively. The rapid promotion of ASEAN-China relations not only initiated but has also become the new engine of regionalism in East Asia.

Many forces and factors underpinned today's regionalisation movement in East Asia. What this article emphasises is that an ASEAN-China relation is the most dynamic bilateral relations in the region. It not only constitutes the most important part of the current East Asian regionalising process, but also serves as a major force and a catalyst to encourage and stimulate Japan and Korea to strengthen their relations with ASEAN countries both economically and politically; this cooperation, in turn, could be developed into a more comprehensive East Asian region-wide effort. Eventually, a real East Asian regionalism or a broader regionalism similar to the East Asian Summit will materialise. Indeed, the development of ASEAN-China bilateral relations has far-reaching regional and global benefits and is contributing to the peace and prosperity of the region.

Appendix: Chronology of ASEAN-China Relations

A simple chronology showing progress made in the past 15 years:

- In July 1991, Chinese Foreign Minister was invited to the opening ceremony of the 24th ASEAN Foreign Ministers' Meeting, marking the start of formal contact between China and ASEAN.
- In July 1994, China attended the first meeting of the ASEAN Regional Forum in Thailand as a consultative partner.
- In April 1995, the first Sino-ASEAN consultation at vice foreign ministerial level was held in Hangzhou, China.
- In July 1996, the ASEAN Standing Committee elevates the status of China from a consultative partner to a full dialogue partner.
- In 1997, China and ASEAN leaders held the first ASEAN-China Summit.
- In 2001, ASEAN and China leaders agreed to establish an ASEAN-China Free Trade Area ("ASEAN-China FTA") by 2010.
- In 2002, ASEAN and China signed the Framework Agreement on Comprehensive Economic Co-Operation.
- In 2002, China and ASEAN signed the Declaration on the Conduct of Parties in the South China Sea and the ASEAN-China Joint Declaration in the Field of Non-Traditional Security Issues.
- In 2003, ASEAN and China signed the Joint Declaration on Strategic Partnership for Peace and Prosperity.
- In 2003, China acceded to the Treaty of Amity and Cooperation (TAC) in Southeast Asia, demonstrating the enhancement of political trust between China and ASEAN.
- In 2003 and 2005, China and ASEAN held Special China-ASEAN Leaders' Meeting on SARS, and Aftermath of Earthquake and Tsunami respectively.
- From 2004, the two parties began implementing the Early Harvest Plan (EHP), cutting tariffs on more than 500 products, as part of the effort to facilitate the birth of the FTA.
- In 2004, the ASEAN-China Plan of Action was signed to implement the Joint Declaration on the ASEAN-China Strategic Partnership for Peace and Prosperity.

- In 2004, ASEAN and China set up a joint working group to study and recommend confidence-building activities to ensure peace and stability in the South China Sea.
- In 2004, the two parties signed a number of agreements on trade in goods and dispute settlement, laying down foundations for standardising tariff cuts and resolving disputes for the birth of FTA.
- From 20 July 2005, China and ASEAN began to cut tariffs on more than 7,000 products, the beginning of a phase of substantial tariff reduction between China and ASEAN in the run-up to the establishment of the FTA.
- The ASEAN-China trade volume reached US$130.37 billion in 2005 and US$160.8 billion in 2006.
- It is expected that the ASEAN-China trade volume will reach US$200 billion by 2010.
- In the past few years, ASEAN and China expanded their cooperation from five to ten priority areas, namely, agriculture, information and communication technology, human resource development, two-way investment, Mekong River Basin development, transportation, energy, culture, tourism and public health.

China's Rise and Its Implications for Mainland Southeast Asia and Laos

Bounnheuang Songnavong

China-ASEAN relations have been improving rapidly after Beijing established diplomatic ties with all Southeast Asian countries in 1991. The relations are based on equality, good neighbourliness and mutual trust and have gone through a process of dialogue, cooperation and strategic partnership. In October 2006, during the ASEAN-China Commemorative Summit held in Nanning, China, leaders from both sides acknowledged that the successful ASEAN-China cooperation in politics and security has strengthened mutual understanding and trust, laying the basis for promoting strategic partnership in peace and prosperity. They also noted that the rapid growth in ASEAN-China relations has brought tangible benefits and have greatly reinforced peace, stability and prosperity in the region. They also welcome China's foreign policy of good neighbourliness. During the summit, ASEAN leaders also reaffirmed their commitment to the "One China policy" and also acknowledged the importance of China's growing market economy for Southeast Asia.

Indeed, for the past 15 years, China has concluded many important agreements with ASEAN to consolidate existing ties and resolve outstanding security issues. For instance, by joining the Treaty of Amity and Cooperation in Southeast Asia (TAC), participating in Asia-Pacific Regional Forum and showing its willingness to accede to the Protocol of the Treaty on the Southeast Asia Nuclear Weapon Free Zone, Beijing has played a leading role in promoting peace and strengthening security in the region. Other measures taken by China have also further improved the security of the region. These include maintaining peace in the Korean Peninsula and improving the security of the South China Sea through the ratification of the Declaration of the Conduct of Parties in the South China Sea. Furthermore, China's willingness to engage and form multilateral forums such as the ASEAN plus Three process, East Asia Summit and the Shanghai Cooperation Organisation, significantly ease the process of expanding its cooperation with ASEAN.

Today, China is bringing its cooperation with ASEAN to another level by supporting the ASEAN Community building efforts, including the Vientiane Action Programme (VAP), the Plan of Action of the ASEAN Security Community, ASEAN Economic Community, ASEAN Socio-Cultural Community and the Initiative for ASEAN Integration (IAI). ASEAN and China are also working closely together to realise a number of programmes for development of the Mekong Basin, such as the Greater Mekong Sub-region (GMS), the ASEAN-Mekong Basin Development Cooperation (AMBDC) and the Mekong River Commission (MRC). Beijing has also taken a number of initiatives to develop the Mekong Basin during the second Sub-regional Summit in Kunming. Some of them include the construction of the Kunming-Bangkok expressway through the territory of Laos and improving navigation along the Mekong River. The aim of these projects is to promote sub-regional integration for sustainable economic development.

China is also increasing its financial assistance to Southeast Asia. For instance, China has recently contributed US$5 billion to the ASEAN Economic Fund in the form of loans for infrastructure development. It has also offered US$1 million to the ASEAN Development Fund (ADF) and another US$1 million for funding two projects of IAI to implement the VAP for bridging the development gap between old and new ASEAN members, including Laos.

Laos-China Bilateral Relations

China-Laos total trade volume is increasing rapidly. From 1991 to 2004, it had grown from US$13 million to US$114 million. However, compared to other mainland Southeast Asian countries, Laos-China total bilateral trade is still relatively small. Nonetheless, by maintaining good relations with China, the Laotian government is aware that it can help promote more multilateral and bilateral cooperation and open up invaluable opportunities for the promotion of peace, prosperity and development in mainland Southeast Asia. The lucrative result of this type of cooperation can be seen in the increase in trading, investment and tourism between mainland Southeast Asian countries and China as generated by the Early Harvest Programme under the framework of the ASEAN-China Free Trade Agreement. China has also introduced cooperative initiatives in other fields such as the expansion of the scope of special preferential tariff treatment for Laos, Cambodia and Myanmar in 2005 and the US$5 million contribution to help improve navigation on the Mekong River along Laos and Myanmar.

The traditional friendship between Laos and China has progressed well and the two sides have achieved a lot in promoting deeper ties and partnership between the two countries and their people and in the ASEAN-China partnership. Nevertheless, the two governments are committed to a long-term friendship and good neighbourhood based on mutual trust and comprehensive cooperation. The Lao people deeply appreciate and are grateful to the selfless support and help offered by the Chinese government and the Chinese people.

In conclusion, a growing China is a complementary contribution to the peace and stability as well as prosperity of mainland Southeast Asia as well as the region. The growth of friendly cooperative relations between ASEAN and China is most encouraging for robust economic growth. The two sides have laid down a solid foundation to enhance future cooperation and are most likely to continue with the dynamic pace of cooperation to further strengthen their evolving strategic partnership.

ASEAN and China are moving towards greater economic integration. The integration is mutually beneficial. Laos appreciates China's fast growing economy. It would like ASEAN and China, all Dialogue Partners and international organisations to provide more effective assistance and support, collectively or individually, to CLMV countries, including Combodia, Laos, Myanmar and Vietnam to accelerate the implementation of VAP and all the initiatives for ASEAN integration. This can help to bridge the development gaps within ASEAN and between ASEAN and other regions.

Bilateral Relations Between China and Myanmar

Aung Kyaw Oo

Myanmar is one of the first few countries to recognise the People's Republic of China after its founding in 1949. Diplomatic relations were established some 57 years ago on 8 June 1950. Since then, both sides have enjoyed good relations and frequent exchanges. In fact, the earliest friendly exchanges between Myanmar and China could be traced back to the Pyu period in Myanmar (100BC to 840AD) when Pyu Crown Prince Sunanda led 35 artists to Tang China (618 AD to 907 AD) for a goodwill visit in 802 AD.

Myanmar and China enjoy a good neighbourly relation that is in line with the five principles of peaceful coexistence. The five principles were put into place in Myanmar-China relations during Premier Zhou Enlai's visit to Myanmar in 1954. They emphasised the following: mutual respect for each other's sovereignty, mutual non-aggression, mutual non-interference in each other's internal affairs, equality and mutual trust, and peaceful co-existence. The Five Principles of Peaceful Coexistence now become norms and principles in international relations. Myanmar-China relations were also referred to as "paukphaw" or a fraternal relationship.

One of the major achievements during the early years of Myanmar-China relations was the settlement of the boundary issue. China and Myanmar shared a common border of more 2,000 km. This made border demarcation a sensitive issue. Nonetheless, the problem was resolved when late Myanmar Prime Minister U Nu and late Chinese Premier Zhou Enlai signed a boundary treaty in October 1960. The boundary treaty is the first one concluded by Myanmar and China with foreign countries on the basis of the five principles of peaceful coexistence. It also paved the way for closer and friendlier ties leading to high-level visits by leaders including Liu Shaoqi, Zhou Enlai, Chen Yi and Deng Xiaoping to Myanmar and Myanmar Prime Minister U Nu to China.

However, Myanmar-China relations were strained after the outbreak of the Cultural Revolution in China in 1967. From 1967 to 1970, an atmosphere of misunderstanding undermined the friendly relations between the two countries. As a result, the Economic and Technical Co-operation Agreement was suspended and Chinese technicians returned home from Myanmar. Both governments recalled their ambassadors and maintained only a low-level diplomatic representation in Yangon and Beijing.

When the Cultural Revolution ended, both sides began restoring relations with the reposting of ambassadors in 1971. Then, at the invitation of Premier Zhou Enlai, General Ne Win, Chairman of the Revolutionary Council, paid a visit to China in August 1971. He was the first head of state to visit China after the Cultural Revolution. His visit marked the rekindling of the spirit of "paukphaw" friendship. Since then, there has been a gradual and consistent development of normal relations between the two countries.

Myanmar-China Relations After 1988

In the wake of the disturbances in 1988 in Myanmar, China continued to maintain its traditional friendship with Myanmar. During Premier Li Peng's visit to Thailand, Australia and New Zealand in November 1988, he made the following remarks in answering a question about China's attitude towards the Government of the Union of Myanmar at a press conference in Bangkok on 13 November 1988:

> China has consistently adhered to a policy of non-interference in the internal affairs of other countries, and Myanmar is no exception. Myanmar is a neighbouring country of China. We hope that the situation there can be stabilised. There exist trade relations between China and Myanmar, which have not been suspended.

Premier Li Peng also reaffirmed Beijing's friendship with Myanmar and upheld cooperation between the two armed forces during a goodwill visit by General Than Shwe in October 1989. He also called for the upholding of the traditional "paukphaw" relations with China.

Since 1988, economic and technical cooperation projects between China and Myanmar have resumed. The construction of the Yangon-Thanlyin Bridge project, which suffered tremendous loss and damage, was resumed. The construction of the National Theatre, which was a gift from President Li Xianian, resumed in January 1989. The construction was completed in January 1991, when Luo Gan, the then Secretary General of the State Council of the PRC visited Myanmar. Bilateral trade between Myanmar and China also resumed and grew rapidly. From 1988 to 2002, it grew more than 300-fold from US$270 million to US$1.1 billion.

In 2000, Vice Chairman of the State Peace and Development Council General Maung Aye and the then Vice President Hu Jintao exchanged official visits to commemorate the golden jubilee of Myanmar-China relations. They signed the "Joint Statement Concerning Framework Document on Future Cooperation in Bilateral Relation between the Union of Myanmar and the People's Republic of China", setting the direction of Myanmar-China partnership for the 21st century.

The milestone agreement was followed by an official visit by President Jiang Zemin from 12 to 15 December 2001. During his visit, President Jiang emphasised the "Paukphaw Sentiments" of the two nations. On 12 December 2001 President Jiang exchanged views with Senior General Than Shwe, Chairman of the State Peace and Development Council, on bilateral relations and issues of mutual interest to both countries. Seven agreements were signed between the two governments during Jiang's visit. General Than Shwe returned President Jiang's visit in January 2003. In October 2006, Prime Minister of the Union of Myanmar General Soe Win attended the 15th Anniversary of China-ASEAN Dialogue Summit held in Nanning, China. He met and had a discussion with Chinese Premier Wen Jiabao.

Myanmar has been deprived of international assistance since 1988, with the exception of China, which has played a major part in Myanmar's economic development. Progress has been made in economic cooperation in the last two years as reflected in the conclusion of over 30 agreements on economic cooperation. In return, Myanmar always adheres to the "One China Policy" and consistently recognises Taiwan as an inseparable part of China's territory.

In conclusion, China and Myanmar have been maintaining long-standing close relations since Tang China and Pyu Myanmar. On the basis of the five principles of peaceful co-existence, Myanmar is strengthening not only its cooperation with China in trade, but its cooperation with ASEAN member countries at a bilateral or multilateral level.

Part III

Economic Relations

China's Economic Growth and Its Impact on the ASEAN Economies

Lu Jianren

China's economy has been expanding rapidly after it adopted the reform and open-door policy in 1978. China's GDP grew more than 15-fold from US$147.3 billion in 1978 to US$2.25 trillion in 2005.[1] Furthermore, from 1979 to 2005, the average increase rate of China's actual GDP was about 9.7 percent (calculated on the basis of comparable price). Per capita GDP increased from US$173 in 1980 to US$1700 in 2005, nearly 10 times higher.

The result of China's high-speed economic growth is also visible on other areas of the Chinese economy. For instance, the structure of China's industry has changed profoundly. In 1978, the primary industry accounted for 28 percent of China's GNP; the secondary industry, 48 percent, and the tertiary industry, 23 percent. By 2005, it was 12 percent, 47 percent and 40 percent for the three industries respectively.[2] This indicates that the industrial structure of China's economy and the quality of the Chinese economy have significantly improved. In addition, China's total trade volume also grew rapidly at an annual rate of over 16 percent from US$20.6 billion in 1978 to US$1.42 trillion in 2005. Furthermore, China's foreign reserves

---

[1] The 1978 data is cited from President Hu Jintao's address at the opening ceremony of the Fortune global forum in Beijing in 2005. The 2005 data is from the State Statistics Bureau.

[2] *Statistical Communique of the People's Republic of China on the 2005 National Economic and Social Development*, released on 28 February 2006.

increased from just US$167 million in 1978 to US$1.2 trillion in 2006 and the impoverished population in rural areas decreased from 250 million to less than 26 million.

The speed of China's economic growth even outpaced the growth experienced by Japan and the Newly Industrialised Economies (NIEs) from the 1970s to the 1990s. As a result, this prompted many to see China as one of the "miracle economies" in Asia.[3] For instance, a report from the United States Department of Agriculture Economic Research Service stated that "no other countries in the world are comparable with China in terms of long-term continuous high-speed growth of the economy. To make the same achievement and changes as made by other countries in decades and even a hundred years, it took China just twenty years".[4]

So what are the main reasons for the high-speed growth of the Chinese economy? Firstly, China enjoys a high investment rate. An important source of China's investment is China's domestic saving, thanks to its very high savings rate. In 1979, the domestic saving rate in China, which was about 32 perccent of its GDP, was already higher than other developing countries. During the 1990s, it increased to about 40 percent before hitting 46 percent in 2005. A major source of China's investment is foreign direct investment (FDI). At the end of 2005, the total volume of cumulative utilised foreign capital in China amounted to US$618 billion. With considerable amounts of domestic and foreign capital, China has successfully avoided the economic slow-down as experienced by most developing countries. By utilising domestic capital and foreign investment, China greatly upgraded its industries and improved its infrastructure, resulting in nearly three decades of strong economic performance. In fact, it was estimated that high investment directly contributed to about 5.5 percent of China's GDP growth rate.[5]

---

[3] In its "golden development period" from 1971 to 1991, Japan's annual economic growth rate was about 9 percent. From 1971 to 2003, the annual growth rate of Korea, Taiwan, and Singapore were 7.06 percent, 7.35 percent, and 6.53 percent, respectively.

[4] Mathew Shane and Fred Gale, "China: A Study of Dynamic Growth," Outlook Report No. (WRS0408), 20 October 2004, http://www.ers.usda.gov.

[5] Ibid.

Secondly, China's low labour cost and abundant supply of cheap labour is also an important factor for the country's economic growth. The labour cost in China is only about 5 percent that of developed countries. This allows China to maintain unparallelled competitiveness in the labour-intensive industry for a long time.

Thirdly, high-speed growth of the Chinese economy was also spurred by the improvement of productivity. The first factor that improved China's productivity is the market economy reform, which resulted in a more effective utilisation of various production elements. The second factor is the transfer of advanced technology and management experience from investing MNCs, host of FDI. The third factor is the development of Chinese education. This value adds to China's labour force, which in turn improved their productivity.

Fourthly, the rapid development of foreign trade also contributed to the country's high economic growth. Although China is a huge country with an equally huge domestic market, China adopted an export-oriented economic strategy in the past 26 years, following the examples of the "export oriented" small countries in East Asia. China's total export is among the largest in the world and is growing faster than imports. In fact, China has been registering trade surplus since 1993, with the amount exceeding US$100 million in 2005. Furthermore, from 2001 to 2005, China's share of gross world trade increased from 4 percent to nearly 7 percent.[6]

Finally, China's continuing economic reform and institutional innovation also contributed to the growth of the Chinese economy. Non-state enterprises have grown rapidly and become the main forces of China's economic growth. As of the end of 2005, the production value of private enterprises and foreign-invested enterprises in China contributed about 65 percent of its GDP. The Ministry of Commerce predicts that it would be increased to about 75 percent by 2010.[7]

---

[6]Wu Qi, "China's Surging Foreign Trade: Joy Tempered with Sorrow," *China Features*, posted at http://www.chinese-embassy.org.uk/eng/zt/Features/t274358.htm

[7]The Ministry of Commerce, "Three Quarters of GDP of China from Private Businesses in Four Years," released on the China News web site (www.chinanews.com.cn) on 12 November 2006.

Thanks to the aforementioned factors, China's economy will continue to grow in the coming 10 to 15 years. In particular, capital and labour, the two factors most important for economic growth, will not experience drastic fluctuation. In this coming period, China will keep its high savings rate and high appeal to foreign capital. In the meantime, the advantage of the relative low labour cost of China will remain unchanged. Most domestic and foreign experts, the World Bank and the IMF believed that as the reform deepens, the Chinese economy would maintain a high growth rate of about 7 to 8 percent till 2020 and would become the largest economy in the world.

Even now, the continuous high growth of the Chinese economy already has made an enormous impact on the rest of the world. According to a study by Chinese scholars, China is the world's largest contributor to global economic growth. Based on statistics from the World Bank, the report showed that from 1990 to 2002 China had the highest contribution rate of about 27 percent, to the GDP increase of the world; the USA, 21 percent, and Japan, a mere 2 percent. During this period, even at its peak, the GDP of China accounted for only 4 percent of the world's total and was far less than those of the USA and Japan; this makes China the biggest contributor to the world's economic growth. Back in the period of 1980-1990, the USA had the highest contribution rate (21 percent) to the increase in the world's GDP; China was second with 12 percent, and Japan third with 10 percent.[8]

Influence of China's Economic Growth on ASEAN Economies

China is not only the locomotive of world economic growth, but also the locomotive of East Asia's economic growth. A report from the World Bank pointed out that the economies in East Asia and ASEAN have experienced strong growth for five years. The average economic growth in the region registered about 8 percent in 2006. With high economic growth, the poverty rate in East Asia dropped sharply. The World Bank report explained that the healthy economic performance

---

[8]Hu Angang, *National Conditions and Development* [*guo qing yu fa zhan*]. Tsinghua University Press, 2006, p. 195.

in the region has a lot to do with China. It stated as follows, "The over 10 percent of China's economic growth laid a good foundation for the overall economic growth of East Asia. The fast growing Chinese economy continues to become an important engine of the entire regional economic growth".[9]

Located in East Asia, China has close economic and trade ties with the East Asian economies. The East Asian economies thus reap considerable benefits from the Chinese economy. For instance, the recovery after 12 years of economic recession in Japan is closely related to its expanded export to and investment in China. Furthermore, China is an important player in reviving and improving the Korean economy especially after overtaking USA to become Korea's largest export market. As for the ASEAN economies, they shared the bonus of the Chinese economic prosperity with the signing of the China-ASEAN free trade agreement (CAFTA) and many bilateral economic agreements.

How does China's economic rise benefit countries in the ASEAN? Firstly, the trade imbalance between China and ASEAN is an important source of economic growth for ASEAN economies. After the dialogue between ASEAN countries and China was established in 1991, bilateral trade between the two sides has been increasing rapidly. Total trade volume increased from US$8 billion in 1991 to US$130.4 billion in 2005, up 16 times and at an annual increase rate of over 20 percent. As of March 2006, both parties became each other's fourth largest trade partner. Specifically, ASEAN is China's third largest import and the fourth largest export market in 2006. More importantly, ASEAN has been registering trade surplus in its trade with China. Particularly, the Philippines, Thailand and Malaysia are constantly listed among the top ten trade deficit sources of China. In 2005, ASEAN-China trade deficit was about US$20 billion and in ASEAN's favour. Despite the huge trade deficit, Chinese Premier Wen Jiabao stated that China will continue to promote its trade with ASEAN.[10]

---

[9]"East Asia Half-Yearly Update — The World Bank Organization," (13 November 2006) in the *International Finance News*, 15 November 2006.

[10]Cited from Premier Wen Jiabao's address at the opening ceremony of The 3rd China-ASEAN Business and Investment Summit, released on the China News website (www.xinhuanet.com) on 31 November 2006.

The continuous increase of trade with China not only boosted the production rate in ASEAN countries, but also created more jobs for the local people. As a result, this contributed to the economic growth in ASEAN countries and helped some ASEAN countries to recover from the 1997 Asian financial crisis. China and ASEAN will continue to build on this trend to improve economic relations and seek greater economic integration especially as the import demands for ASEAN goods from the USA and Japan weaken. This development prompted Philippines President Gloria Macapagal Arroyo to state, "With China, we have less reliance on the markets of the West."[11] China-ASEAN bilateral trade is anticipated to exceed US$200 billion by the end of 2008.

Secondly, China's economic initiatives in ASEAN, which were carved out as a bid to quell fears of its rising, have brought many economic benefits to ASEAN economies. One good example is the CAFTA. Although it is still taking gradual effect, its "Early Harvest Programme" has significant effects on ASEAN's agricultural sector. China also unilaterally cut import tax for ASEAN's agricultural products, particularly those from less developed economies such as Laos, Cambodia and Myanmar to help out these economies. China's trade initiatives and concession have led ASEAN economies to register high trade surplus in their trade with China. In 2005, ASEAN's trade surplus in its agricultural trade with China amounted to over US$2 billion[12] with Indonesia, Malaysia and Thailand enjoying the largest trade surplus. As the implementation of CAFTA picks up speed, other tax reduction in sensitive agricultural products such as rubber would further benefit ASEAN economies.

Thirdly, the strengthening of the Chinese economy is slowly leading state-owned and private enterprises in China to invest abroad especially in ASEAN. In the first half of 2006, the total investment of Chinese enterprises in ASEAN was about US$1.3 billion. This is small compared to ASEAN's total investment in China, which is about

---

[11]Cited from Philippines President Gloria Macapagal Arroyo's address at the opening ceremony of The 3rd China-ASEAN Business and Investment Summit, released on the China News web site (www.xinhuanet.com) on 31 November 2006.

[12]Refer to the article "Analysis of CAFTA Agricultural Trade Interest," on the *International Business Daily*, 13 July 2006.

US$40 billion. However, this situation is gradually changing especially after the Chinese government implemented the "go abroad" strategy to encourage more Chinese enterprises to invest overseas. The Chinese government has also set up a US$5 billion fund to provide loans for Chinese enterprises going overseas. In addition, ASEAN's rich natural resources such as oil, natural gas and timber, which are strongly complementary to China's economy, are also attracting investment from Chinese enterprises.

Indeed, in recent years, China's investment in the ASEAN registered an annual increase of about 60 percent. Currently, Chinese enterprises have funded the establishment of nearly 1,000 non-financial enterprises in the ten ASEAN countries. Furthermore, investment areas have been expanded from previous small projects in the processing, assembly and manufacturing sectors to big projects in industries such as construction, hotel, electrical and electronics, mining and transportation. The investment forms have changed from direct investment to technical investment, BOT (Building–Operation–Transfer) and other forms. Enterprises with Chinese investment have contributed to local employment, taxation and economy.

Chinese investment in ASEAN will likely continue as the China-ASEAN Free Trade Area will provide more favourable tax policies to Chinese enterprises that invest in ASEAN. Besides, both China and ASEAN are now negotiating an investment agreement. Both sides are also discussing about setting up a number of economic trade cooperation zones in the ASEAN region to facilitate more intra-investment. These zones will feature ready infrastructure, complete industry chain, high relevance and strong driving and radiating capability.

Fourthly, as China's economy continues to grow, China will pump more resources into strengthening the capacity building of ASEAN countries and benefitting the local peoples.

In order to follow through the long-term strategy of building "an amicable, tranquil and prosperous neighbourhood", China will strive to build good relations with ASEAN, an important neighbour and strategic partner. Especially, China feels obligated to assist less developed ASEAN countries such as Cambodia, Laos, Myanmar, and to some extent Vietnam, with their economic development. The first method is to strengthen the capacity building of these countries. In recent years, China and ASEAN made significant achievements in this aspect by providing human resource training, economic technical aid and cooperation in various areas. For example, China has trained over 6,000 talents in different fields for the ASEAN countries. The number of trained talents, nevertheless, is still inadequate for satisfying the requirements of ASEAN countries.

The other method is to offer foreign aid. Although China is still a developing country and has limited foreign aid capability, it was able to arrange a number of foreign aid projects in less developed ASEAN countries. For example, from 1998 to 2005, China had provided about US$1.2 billion in loans and aid to Laos. Furthermore, in November 2005, when President Hu Jintao visited Vietnam, he offered Vietnam a development aid package worth US$1 billion for the construction of power plants and other infrastructure projects in the country.[13] China has also arranged many foreign aid projects with old ASEAN members such as Indonesia, Thailand and the Philippines. In the coming years, China will continue to provide more training programmes as well as financial aid and loans to help bring prosperity and development to ASEAN.

Fifthly, by keeping Chinese currency *Renminbi* strong in the long term China will contribute to the stability of regional currencies including those of ASEAN countries. In 1997 when the Asia financial crisis broke out China did not depreciate *Renminbi* even though it was also in a difficult situation. Southeast Asian economies were thus saved from another economic crisis. Now China has a foreign currency reserves of US$1 trillion. With a strong *reminbi* and the gradual appreciation, China is in a position to contribute more to regional currency stability. Currently, East Asia has a currency exchange mechanism under the Chiang Mai Initiative (CMI). In 2005, China and Indonesia signed the currency exchange agreement under the CMI framework. It is beneficial to the financical stability of the region. With *Renminbi* as a

---

[13]The figures are from the article "Economic Wrestle on the Indo-China Peninsula," of the *South Winds* [*nan feng chuang*] magazine, 30 May 2006.

strong and internationally influential currency in East Asia, it is good for the economy, trade and finance of the region, including ASEAN. The appreciation of *Renminbi* has a positive effect on China-ASEAN trade cooperation. The increase in *Renminbi* exchange rate could lower the export price of products from ASEAN to China, an incentive for Chinese enterprises to invest in ASEAN to take advantage of the higher purchasing power of the *Renminbi* abroad. At the same time, some ASEAN countries can reduce their trade deficit with China.

Finally, China's economic growth has become one of the main driving forces for regional integration, and this is helping the development of the ASEAN Economic Community and East Asian regionalism. As its economy has become larger and wields greater leverage in the region, China can play a bigger role in the regional integration process. Utilising its increasing influence China has played an active and constructive role. China is a keen member of other multilateral regional framework such as the ASEAN+3 and the East Asian Summit. It also supports the core role of the ASEAN in East Asia integration and the building of the ASEAN Economic Community. The establishment of the ASEAN Economic Community also requires the construction of the hardware environment and various sub-regional schemes of economic cooperation. In this regard, China has been very active in participating in a series of sub-regional economic cooperation programmes such as the Lancangjiang River-Mekong River drainage area, Indonesia-Malaysia-Thailand Growth Triangle, Brunei-Indonesia-Indonesia-the Philippines East ASEAN Growth Zone, Cambodia-Myanmar-Laos-Vietnam Economic Development Zone, and the "Two Corridors and One Economic Circle" between Vietnam and China. As China's economy is one of the biggest in the East Asian region, it is important that China continues to be involved in these regional and sub-regional cooperation mechanisms.

Bright Prospects for China-ASEAN Relations

China's phenomenal economic growth for the past decade has greatly helped to sustain economic growth and development in the region and to advance regional economic integration. In the next 15 years, the Chinese economy will continue to grow and bring more economic benefits to the people in China and the region, while regional economic integration will deepen and ASEAN will develop into a strong community. As strategic partners, China and ASEAN can join hands in building a peaceful and prosperous tomorrow.

China-Singapore Investment Relations: New Development and Prospect

Zhao Hong

In recent years, due to some positive factors such as good political and diplomatic relations and rapid economic growth, China-Singapore's economic relation has been developing faster than ever before. In terms of investment relations, Singapore is the earliest among ASEAN countries to invest in China and the most efficient. Compared to the 1980s and 1990s, Singapore's current investments in China have been experiencing some new changes and development. This article examines the new features and development trends of Singapore's investments in China. It also analyses the prospects of bilateral investment relations between the two countries before concluding that the two countries should further exploit their respective comparative advantages, and collaborate to invest in other ASEAN countries and elsewhere.

Brief Review of Bilateral Investment Relations

As one of the East Asian newly industralised economies (NIEs), Singapore relies heavily on international trade, finance and foreign direct investment (FDI) for its economic development. It has emerged as a regional source of FDI since the second half of the 1980s when it became a net lender of capital funds. Although Singapore's investments in China began in the late 1970s, most of the investments were in ASEAN countries with Malaysia as the top host country. China was not a main destination and only ranked sixth in the number of companies set up, and tenth in the amount of investment in 1990.[1] However, Singapore's investments in China substantially increased after 1990, following the establishment of diplomatic relations and the encouragement from the Singapore government. In the mid 1990s, Singapore's investments in China experienced a peak period (Figure 1). During this period, Singapore's investments were mainly located in southeast coastal cities, such as Shanghai, Fuzhou, Xiamen, Shantou, Shenzhen, Guangzhou and Zhuhai, and in construction (48 percent) and manufacturing (42 percent). In 1997, China overtook Malaysia to become Singapore's top investment destination in cumulative terms.

At the turn of the 21st century, Singapore's investments in China saw a new development in terms of quality and quantity. China became a major destination of Singapore's investment in Asia (Table 1). According to the Ministry of Trade and Industry of Singapore, in 2004, the accumulation of Singapore's investment in China was US$21 billion, accounting for 25 percent of its total investments in Asia; in 2005, it increased to US$28 billion.[2] Currently Singapore is China's 6th largest foreign investor, behind Hong Kong, Taiwan, the USA, EU and Japan, and the largest for ASEAN.

After China's "go out strategy" in 2002, more and more Chinese enterprises started to invest in Southeast Asia, including Singapore. During the 1990s, Chinese enterprises in Singapore were mostly big state-owned enterprises in the trade, petroleum, transportation and banking sectors. After 2002, private enterprises made their foray into Singapore as well as other ASEAN countries. The investments of these enterprises covered various sectors such as electronic, information technology (IT) and information equipment. According to ASEAN Secretariat statistics, from 1995 to 2004, the accumulated value of Chinese investment in ASEAN countries was over US$1 billion while the accumulated value of Chinese investment in Singapore was US$224.4 million or 22 percent of its total investments in ASEAN.[3]

---

[1]*Business Times*, 22 September 1992.
[2]Information provided by Ministry of Trade and Industry of Singapore at http://app. mti.gov.sg.
[3]ASEAN Secretariat-ASEAN FDI Database, 2005.

Figure 1. Chinese FDI in Singapore (1995–2004) (US$ milllion)

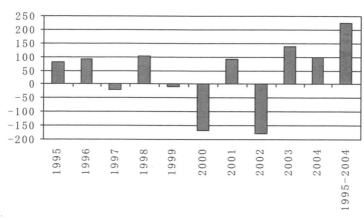

Source: ASEAN Secretariat-ASEAN FDI Database, 2005.

Table 1. Major Destinations of Singapore's Investments in Asia (Stock at year-end, US$ million)

	2003	Percentage (%)	2004	Percentage (%)
Asia	77,582	100	84,963	100
ASEAN	34,874	45	37,981	44.7
Malaysia	13,593	17.5	13,904	16.4
Indonesia	10,319	13.4	11,820	14
Thailand	4,706	6	6,708	9
Mainland China	19,820	25.6	20,907	25
Hong Kong	11,243	14.5	11,558	13.6
Taiwan	3,688	4.8	3,696	4.4

Source: Ministry of Trade and Industry of Singapore, http://app.mti.gov.sg

The number of Chinese enterprises investing in Singapore increased from 859 in 2001 to 1671 in 2005, ahead of India, Australia, New Zealand and South Korea (Table 2). Singapore has become an important "springboard" for Chinese enterprises going overseas.

Table 2. Number of Asia-Pacific Enterprises in Singapore (2001–2005)

Country	2001	2002	2003	2004	2005
Australia and New Zealand	816	921	1050	1182	1424
China	859	958	1160	1432	1671
India	1121	1260	1441	1526	1644
South Korea	281	322	375	433	446
Total	3077	3461	4026	4573	5185

Source: http://www.edb.gov.sg/edb/sg/zh-cn/indes.html

Figure 2. Bilateral Trade between China and Singapore (2000–September 2006) (US$ billion)

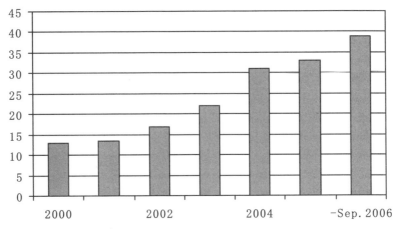

Source: Ministry of Commerce of China, http://countryreport.mofcom.gov.cn/.

The development of bilateral investments between China and Singapore also promoted the growth of bilateral trade. According to the Commercial Ministry of China, the total value of bilateral trade between the two countries reached US$20 billion in 2003 and further increased to over US$30 billion in 2005 before hitting nearly US$40 billion for the first ten months of 2006 and accounting for over 10 percent of Singapore's total foreign trade (Figure 2). Singapore was the 7th largest international trade partner of China and the first among ASEAN countries.

New Development and Features of Singapore's Investments in China

As China's foreign investment policies change and regional economic integration develops, the investment models and structures of Singapore's investments in China likewise went through a transformation. Comparing Singapore's recent investments in China with those of the 1990s, the changes and new trends are more distinct, reflecting that foreign investment in China has entered a new stage.

1. New Investment and Cooperation Models

Before 2000, Singapore companies' investments in China mainly took the form of joint ventures and project co-operation. FDI formed the main part of Singapore's investments in China.

As China's economy becomes more internationalised and investment management better established, Singapore's companies began investing in China through the merging and purchasing of local enterprises. Venture investment and enterprise purchases also became important models of investment and cooperation in China. For example, Singapore Vertext Venture Holdings (祥峰集团) entered China by venture investment some years ago, and its investment targets are mainly Chinese state-owned enterprises. The company's eventual purpose is to reform these state-owned enterprises and have them listed on stock markets. It has been quite successful in this field, and has developed into a complex company with its business fields covering electronics, communication, IT and software and life science.

Another example is Singapore Vanda Group (中联系统), a software company headquartered in Hong Kong. It is also the largest commercial partner of IBM in Southeast Asia. It announced that its development strategy in China is to transfer its management, technology and information resources in Singapore to its branch companies in China, and transfer its technicians and creative manpower in China to Southeast Asia, thus establishing its network and promoting its business between China and Southeast Asia. It is believed that as the Chinese economy becomes more global-oriented, this kind of cooperation model will be further extended between China and Singapore.

Another new phenomenon is that more and more Chinese companies have been listed in Singapore's stock market. By the end of 2005, over 80 Chinese enterprises were listed in the Singapore stock market, with market share value of about S$16 billion and total capital raised to approximately S$2.6 billion. To be listed in foreign stock markets has become another important means for Chinese companies to raise capital abroad. One of the main reasons for the increasing number of Chinese listed enterprises in Singapore is the encouragement of both governments (China and Singapore). The Chinese government supports domestic enterprises to go overseas to expedite the establishment of modern enterprises and improve their competitive edge. On the other hand, the Singapore government wants to bandwagon on the Chinese economy, which shows great potential after its World Trade Organisation (WTO) accession.

2. Changing Investment Distributions

As mentioned earlier, in the 1990s, most of Singapore's investments were in southeast China. For instance, in 1993, its FDI in Fujian accounted for over 30 percent of its total FDI in China and its FDI in Guangdong accounted for 16 percent of its total FDI in China[4] As more Singapore enterprises have been changing from labour-intensive companies to capital- and technology-intensive companies, their investments in China have been "going north", pursuing better investment environments, including hard and soft conditions. As Table 3 shows, Jiangsu and Shanghai have overtaken Fujian and Guangdong to become Singapore's top investment destination, accounting for nearly half of its total FDI in China. Furthermore, as the northeastern and western developmental programmes are implemented, these areas have also been attracting Singapore's investments. In 2003, a "Singapore City" was established in Shenyang. By the end of 2005, the accumulation value of Singapore's investments in Shenyang had reached over US$300 million, involving more than 200 projects. By the end of 2005, the total value of

---

[4]D. Lu and G. Zhu, "Singapore Foreign Direct Investment in China: Features and Implications," *ASEAN Economic Bulletin*, Vol. 12, No.1, 1995.

Table 3. Geographical Distribution of Singapore's
FDI In China (%)

	1993	2004
Jiangsu & Shanghai	19.0	45
Guangdong	16.0	14
Shandong	10.4	11
Fujian	30.3	9
Zhejiang	–	8
Others	25.3	13
Total	100	100

Source: *China's Statistics Year Book*, China's Statistics
Press, 2005. The figures of 1993 are from D. Lu and G.
Zhu (1995).

Singapore's investments in Liaoning province had reached nearly
US$2 billion. Furthermore, in recent years, more and more "modern
agricultural parks" have appeared in central and western provinces of
China. Many of them are invested by Singaporeans.

In terms of industrial distribution, although Singapore's investments
in China still focus on manufacturing sectors and real assets, its
investments in high technology, service sectors and environmental
protection have increased rapidly.

3. *China as Singapore's Production Base*

In the past, like many other multinational firms, the main purpose of
Singapore's investments in China was to take advantage of China's
abundant labour and natural resources. They viewed China as an
important base to reduce their production costs and raise their
international competitiveness. This phenomenon, however, has changed
since the late 1990s.

Now more and more Singapore companies have taken their
investments in China as a core part of their globalisation strategy
rather than to process products and reduce costs. For instance, the
Singapore Telecom announced that its purpose of entering the Chinese
market was not to occupy this market. Its main strategy is to induce its

overseas customers and partners to invest in this country so that they could take advantage of the facilities of its host partners and to enlarge its business network in the Asia-Pacific region. The main customers of Singapore Telecom in China include ABB group, Citibank and other well-known multinational firms.

4. Investments in China as Singapore's Main Interest Resources and Driving Forces

For instance, Temasek Holdings announced recently that its total investments in China amounted to S$7.5 billion, and investment in China has been an essential part of its business. Its investments in China cover banking and financial sector, energy and resources, transport and logistics, telecoms and media, pharmacy and health care. Another example is Hong Leong Asia Limited (亚洲丰隆) which began its investment in China in 1994. Now it has developed into a complex industrial group, with its core business in China. The value of its business in China accounts for over 80 percent of the total value of its whole business.

5. Decrease in government intervention

The rapid increase in Singapore's investments in China in the 1990s should be attributed to the active role played by the Singapore government. During that time, senior officials made a number of visits to China to enhance goodwill between the two countries and paved the way for Singapore investors. For instance, Minister Mentor Lee Kuan Yew visited many places in China to build connections with state and local officials, and personally chose the places for Singapore investors. The Singapore government was also involved in investments through government linked companies, such as Temasek Holdings and its affiliated companies like Singapore Power, Capitaland. Now that Singapore investors in China have become more experienced and matured, the Singapore government changed its role to indirect involvement with the aim of promoting investments through market mechanism. For instance, the Singapore government has renamed the

Trade Development Board to "International Enterprise Singapore" (IE Singapore), to establish "Business Support Office" in China and "Network China" for the provision of services and information to private enterprises for their investments in China.[5]

Prospects of China-Singapore's Investment Relations

In recent years, China's strategies to introduce foreign capital have developed to a new stage, emphasising quality rather than quantity of foreign investments. The main purpose of introducing foreign capital is to bring more advanced technology and management skills to promote the reform of domestic enterprises and the development of socialist market economy, rather than simply to increase more capital inflow.

Singapore is a newly developed country in Asia, and has good political and cultural relations with China. The Chinese governments at all levels have increased their efforts to extend cooperation with Singapore. Many provinces have set up bilateral investment promotion councils with Singapore, and have newly established many science and technology parks such as Hangzhou-Singapore Industrial Park and Chendu-Singapore Industrial Park. There is great potential for further bilateral investment relations between these two countries.

1. Venture Investment

Venture investment and enterprise purchase have become an important investment model in China in recent years. For China, venture investment from foreign countries does not merely mean capital inflows to China; more importantly and essentially, it is to promote enterprise-reforms and enhance the productivity of state-owned capital in China. China has over eight million small- and medium-sized enterprises, accounting for 99 percent of its total enterprises. Many of them, especially state-owned enterprises, are facing many problems such

---

[5]Liang Luo-bing, "Policy Factor in Overseas Investment in China: a Case Study of Singapore and Taiwan," *Journal of Contemporary Asia-Pacific*, Chinese Academy of Social Science, 2006.

as capital shortage, backward management, low technology and low efficiency. They badly need institutional reform and cooperation with foreign enterprises.

Singapore is one of the 15 largest enterprise-purchase countries in the world. It is experienced in international venture investment. Currently, it has over 150 capital management companies, managing venture investment funds of over S$16 billion. In 2001, Singapore's exchange value of international enterprise purchase was over US$10 billion. China is a potential market for Singapore's venture investment.

2. Project and Construction Management

The concept of project and construction management is still new in China and few foreign companies have invested in this field. As a big developing country, China spent billions of dollars on various construction projects such as large factories, bridges, skyscrapers, highways and other infrastructures. As the criteria and demand for quality control rise, more and more people realised the importance and necessity of project and construction management. This has created a new field of investment in China.

Singapore has its advantages on this aspect and has many professional companies. For instance, Singapore CPG Corporation (新加坡工程管理公司) is one of Asia's leading development and management professionals. Its investment programmes cover project management, design, construction management, facilities management and quality assurance testing for buildings and infrastructure projects. Singapore CPG Corporation has expanded its business to China. It is undoubted that Singapore will give full play to its advantages in this field.

3. IT Sectors

China's entry into WTO has enlarged its IT market. The Chinese government spent millions of dollars on the IT sector every year. As Chinese economy develops, the demand for education increases. In fact,

E-education is fast becoming an emerging industry in China. It has created good opportunities for foreign investment in China.

As a newly developed country, Singapore has its investment advantages in IT sectors. Singapore Crimsonlogic is one of the leading IT service providers and has expanded its business to China. Its main products include TradeNet, Electronic Filing System, E-Stamping and TradePalette. Both governments should take effective measures to encourage Singapore's investments in E-business, E-government and E-education, thus promoting China-Singapore economic cooperation to a higher stage.

4. Investments in Central and Western Regions

Although Singapore's investments in China have made some achievements, there still exist some problems. For instance, the investment scales are still limited and decentralised as compared to those of Japan, the USA and EU in China. Singapore should establish new advantages and concentration. It is significant and in accordance with the principle of comparative advantages to further encourage Singapore's investments in China's central and western regions where competitions are not so fierce.

Singapore is an agricultural-importing country. In recent years, Singapore has been enlarging its investment in agricultural sectors abroad. China's central and western regions are rich in agricultural resources. After several years of development, the infrastructures and investment environments there have been improved greatly. As the strategy of "building a socialist countryside" is implemented, these regions will be further developed with the potential for foreign investments. In fact, some Singaporean companies have already started to invest in these regions and established many "modern agricultural parks" to develop ecological tourism there. Singapore-based Wilmar recently announced a US$4.3 billion merger plan that would create Asia's largest agribusiness group and leading merchandiser and processor of edible oils and agricultural products in China. Indeed, Singapore can play its role and form its new advantages in these regions.

Exploring New Fields of Cooperation

Singapore's investments in China have entered a new stage, and the future of China's investments in ASEAN and Singapore are bright. But the bilateral investment relations still do not correspond with the status of these two countries in terms of economic development and potential. There remains great space for further cooperation. The governments of these two countries should exploit their respective comparative advantages and make efforts to further promote bilateral economic cooperation. The following are some suggestions for the above:

1. Singapore's investments should focus on potential sectors such as venture investment, project and construction management and IT sectors, and to move its investment to China's central and western parts.

2. The Singapore government should further reduce its intervention and change its role accordingly. The government had played an important role at the initial stage of Singapore's investments in China. Personal links and governmental assurance did reduce uncertainties and risks in the international business and hence expedite investment. But it should be said that it is the economic factors such as industrial sectors, investment scales and environment, rather than political factors that determine the efficiency and success of investment. The experience of Singapore's investment in China shows that government's behaviour can affect business location choice and other investment decisions, but it cannot and should not take the place of market mechanism in the long term.

3. China and Singapore should collaborate to invest in under-developed countries. China implemented its "go out strategy" in 2002, and many state-owned and private enterprises were encouraged to invest abroad. As China moves from a lower stage to a higher stage of development, it is inevitable that its outward investment tends to grow. China has foreign currency reserves of US$1 trillion and is ready to invest overseas. But China is still less experienced in venturing abroad. On the part of Singapore, as a newly industrialised country, Singapore has both the physical capital and human capital that China craves for.

If these two countries can collaborate to invest in an under-developed country, it goes without saying that new fields for cooperation can be further explored.

Singapore's Relations with China

Teng Siow Song

China's relations with Southeast Asia, traditionally called *Nanyang* (South Seas) by the Chinese, are extensive and deep-rooted in history, geography and migration. Geographically, Singapore was part of the "Pan-Malayan lands". Trade between China and Pan-Malaya dates back to the early centuries. A fair amount of trade was recorded as early as the Tang Dynasty (618–907). The early trade activities were often mixed with tribute-bearing missions, a peculiar Chinese way of conducting diplomacy with smaller states in *Nanyang*. Regular and steady growth in trade started only after the second part of the 19th century, with the increased influx of Chinese immigrant labour into British Malaya.

In fact, the Chinese had frequented the Malay lands long before the Portuguese conquered Malacca in 1511. In 1349, a Chinese trader gave a vivid account of life in Temasek, the name of old Singapore. In 1409, Admiral Zheng He led an expedition to Malacca and made it one of China's tributary states. However, it was not until 1819 when the British East India Company established a settlement in Singapore that sizeable Chinese communities began to grow.

By 1860, ethnic Chinese constituted 60 percent of Singapore's total population of 82,000, 15 percent of Malacca's 67,000 and nearly 30 percent of Penang's 67,000. Most Chinese mainly from Fujian and Guangdong provinces of China migrated to Malaya under the contract-labour system. But they soon became traders and craftsmen and eventually dominated the economic life of the Straits Settlements.

After the formation of the Peoples' Republic of China in 1949, China's relations with Southeast Asia assumed new dimensions, with complex ideological and geo-political forces coming into play. This gave rise to more than two decades of Cold War relations. It was not until the early 1970s with the advent of international détente that individual Southeast Asian countries started to normalise relations with China. Singapore formalised its diplomatic relations with China only in October 1990.

Looking back, Singapore's relations with China had also been guided by a high sense of pragmatism. In separating trade from politics, pragmatism had enabled China-Singapore relations to survive in the Cold War period. When China's trade with Indonesia, the Philippines and Thailand was either seriously disrupted or banned altogether, China's trade with Singapore continued uninterrupted. Most remarkably, for four decades from 1950 to 1990, Sino-Singapore trade was conducted in the absence of a formal diplomatic framework.

East Asia's Trade Relations with China

Trade is typically one of the most important factors linking bilateral and multilateral relations between countries. Accordingly, the East Asian region has already developed a fairly high level of intra-regional trade. In 2004, the East Asian region absorbed about 47 percent of Japan's total exports; 43 percent of China's total exports; 47 percent of Korea's exports; 60 percent of Taiwan's exports; 59 percent of Hong Kong's exports; 55 percent of Singapore's exports and 43 percent of the average exports of the ASEAN-4.

In the early 2000s, China was mostly referred to as a rising regional economic power operating a regional economic growth engine. By 2005, China's economy had reached a new turning point whereby its domestic production, consumption and foreign trade had, for the first time, started to exert a significant impact on the world economy. On account of its rapid industrial expansion, China has become the world's top consumer of a wide variety of natural resources and primary commodities from steel and aluminium to oil and gas; its rising demand for these products had driven up their world prices. For instance, the recent oil price hike was attributed to China's increased demand for oil as China has now become the world's second largest consumer of oil. For boom or for bust, the movement of the Chinese economy has started to become either a positive or a potential disruptive force for the global economy.[1]

Regional Impact of China's Rise

China's economic growth actually fits in quite well with the overall East Asian growth patterns. Since the East Asian region absorbs about 50% of China's exports and supplies about 60 percent of China's FDI, it is not hard to explain why China's rapidly growing economy since 1978 has impacted significantly on many East Asian economies to their mutual benefit. However, the actual impact of the fast-growing Chinese economy on the East Asian economies has been quite uneven. China's dynamic economic growth has produced both positive and negative effects on individual East Asian economies in the region. Japan and the four NIEs were able to benefit immensely from China's open-door policy with their export of capital and technology to China.

In contrast, China and the ASEAN economies tend to be more competitive than complementary. In some ways, China's dynamic economic growth has exerted strong competitive pressure on the ASEAN economies, which are vying for FDI with China as a competitor as well as competing head-on with China's manufacturing exports in the developed country markets.[2]

On the other hand, a recent study by UNCTAD confirms that China's growth has not adversely affected FDI inflow to other East Asian economies. Furthermore, China "appears to be crowding in rather than crowding out FDI in the region."[3]

---

[1]For further discussion, see John Wong, "China's Economy in 2004: Stability Takes Precedence over Growth," *EAI Background Brief No. 222.* Singapore: East Asian Institute, National University of Singapore, 10 January 2005.

[2]For further discussion on this topic, see Prakash Loungani, "Comrades or Competitors? Trade Links between China and Other East Asian Economies," *Finance & Development,* June 2000, pp. 34–36.

[3]"China is Not Crowding out FDI from the Rest of East Asia, Experts Say," *Information Note* (Press Information 2005), UNCTAD/PRESS/IN/2005/007. 07/03/05, posted at http://www.unctad.org/Templates/Webflyer.asp?docID=5795&intItemID=1634&lang=1.

Still, many ASEAN economies were watching the recent economic rise of China with apprehension, particularly in the aftermath of the Asian financial crisis. While many ASEAN countries were plagued by persistent economic crises and domestic political instability, China in recent years has been intent on its single-minded pursuit of economic modernisation. This has resulted in the further narrowing of development gaps between ASEAN and China, adding to ASEAN's fears that they might be left behind by China's continuing economic growth.

However, China's dynamic economic growth since the early 2000s has started to transform China's economic relations with ASEAN and East Asia. On account of China's vast size and diversity and compounded by its high speed growth, the rise of China has not just ushered in the third wave of East Asia's growth and integration, but also rendered the third wave to be politically and economically more significant than the previous two. In a short span of a few years, China's levels of production, consumption and trade have risen to such high levels that they have started to exert far greater impact on, not just the regional, but global economy.

Take China's trade relations with ASEAN (see Figure 1). In recent years, China has become the top trade partner of most of its neighbouring economies. China's unique pattern of trade balance with its major trading partners has been the major driving force behind the region's economic growth and integration. Figure 2 shows that, as in the past few years, China in 2005 continued to run substantial trade deficits with its neighbouring economies, from Japan, Korea, Taiwan and ASEAN-5 to Australia and India. China turned around by incurring a large trade surplus with the United States and the EU. In this way, China could still end up with an overall trade surplus. China's trade deficits with its neighbours also mean that China has opened up its vast domestic market for their exports (both manufactured products and primary commodities), thereby operating as an engine for their economic growth.

In the past, many ASEAN countries were apprehensive of a rising China because of its potential competitive pressure on ASEAN's manufactured exports and the zero-sum effect on ASEAN's FDI (i.e., more FDI to China means less to ASEAN). But the global trade-FDI-

Figure 1. China's Trade with ASEAN 6 (1980–2005)

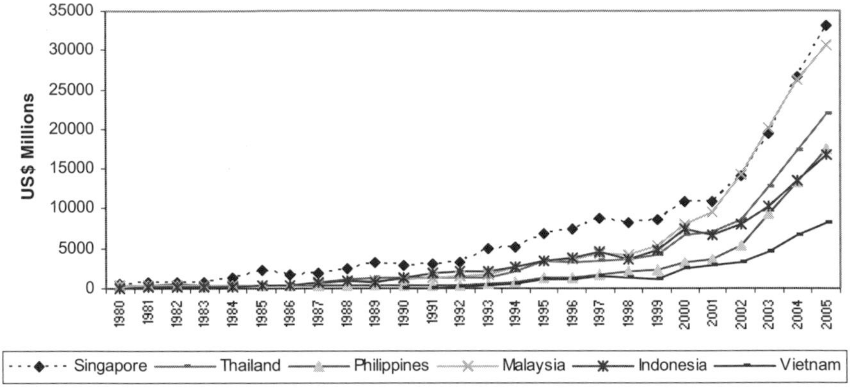

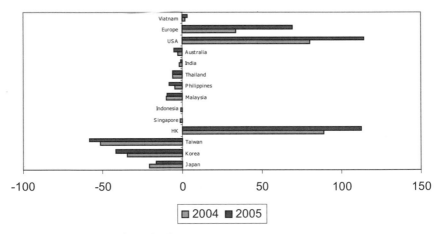

Source: *China Statistical Yearbook*, various years.

Figure 2. China's Trade Balance wih Selected Countries (in US$ billions) (2004–2005)

Source: *China Statistical Yearbook*, various years.

technology linkages have since radically been transformed with the rise of global and regional production networks. Now with China and other East Asian economies becoming increasingly integrated into many common international supply chains, the rise of China has suddenly turned into a win-win phenomenon for the East Asian region, particularly for the fast-growing ASEAN economies.

Viewed from a different angle, China's export engine operates not just as a source of its own economic growth, but also as a catalyst for regional and global economic integration. In this way, China's export sector has built a vital economic relationship not just with the ASEAN economies but also with the global economy at large.

China's FTA Initiative

At the ASEAN-China Summit in November 2001, former Chinese Premier Zhu Rongji proposed the creation of a free trade area between China and ASEAN within 10 years. On 4 November 2002, China and the ASEAN countries signed a framework agreement in Cambodia to establish an FTA by 2010.[4] To show its serious intention and to expedite the process, China on 1 January 2004 initiated the Early Harvest Programme with some ASEAN countries, cutting tariffs on 500 items of mainly agricultural products.

The formation of the ASEAN-China FTA signifies the creation of an economic region of 1.7 billion consumers with a combined GDP of US$2 trillion. It offers an effective means for smaller ASEAN states to overcome its disadvantage of smallness by pooling resources and combining markets. This will in time lead to greater economic integration between China and ASEAN, clearly a win-win situation for both sides.[5] The perceived China economic threat turned into an opportunity for ASEAN.

With China continuing its dynamic economic growth, opportunities will certainly arise for the ASEAN countries to gain a foothold in China's growing market. Apart from its primary commodities, ASEAN's resource-based products will be in great demand in China. The recent years have witnessed an upsurge of ASEAN's exports of natural resource products to China to satisfy the voracious demands of

---

[4]The framework agreement signed by the 11 nation states sets out a road map for trade liberalisation in goods and services for most countries by 2010 and for the less developed ASEAN nations (namely Cambodia, Laos, Myanmar and Vietnam) by 2015.

[5]For further discussion on this topic, see John Wong and Sarah Chan, "China-ASEAN Free Trade Agreement: Shaping Future Economic Relations," *Asian Survey*, Vol. XLIII, No. 3, May/ June 2003, pp. 507–526.

its manufacturing sector. China is such a vast and disparate market that East China, South China and Southwest China can individually offer different opportunities to different ASEAN producers. Not surprisingly, by the end of 2005, China-ASEAN two-way trade had surpassed US$130 billion, with ASEAN becoming one of China's largest trading partners.[6] In 2005, ASEAN was China's 4th largest trade partner while China was the grouping's 5th largest trade partner.

In the years to come, as the China-ASEAN FTA scheme is gradually phased in, multinationals in the region will gradually restructure their supply chains and rationalise their production networks by taking China and ASEAN together as a single market. This will eventually lead to a reshuffling of regional production networks and hence a redistribution of the regional FDI flows. The new regional production patterns will be based on a bigger and more diverse market. In short, both trade and FDI in the region should continue to grow under the impact of the ASEAN-China FTA. And this will certainly be a win-win outcome for both sides.

Of equal importance, Premier Wen at the Summit also signed the Treaty of Amity and Cooperation (TAC) with ASEAN in order to express China's intention of establishing a strategic partnership with ASEAN for "peace and prosperity."[7] China is the first country to conclude this historic treaty and this signalled to the ASEAN countries, her acceptance of ASEAN's norms and values, and her willingness to play by the rules as a responsible regional and global leader. In other words, "China wants to be seen as a responsible member of the international community."[8]

More Good Years

Since 1978, when Chinese paramount leader Deng Xiaoping started economic reform and initiated the open-door policy, China's approach

---

[6]*China Monthly Statistics*, December 2005.

[7]"ASEAN, China Forge Strategic Partnership," posted at http://www.chinaview.cn on 8 October 2003.

[8]See Isagani de Castro, "China snuggles up to Southeast Asia," posted at http://www.atimes.com.

Figure 3. Economic Growth in Southeast Asia (1981–2005)

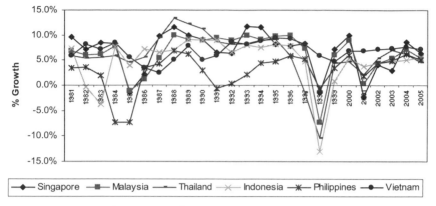

Source: John Wong, author's various compilations.

to foreign relations has also become pragmatic. This led to further growth of the two-way relations between China and ASEAN in general and between China and Singapore in particular. Singapore expanded economic ties with China, especially after Deng's tour of South China (*Nanxun* in 1992). By 2005, Singapore, despite being a very small country, had become China's seventh largest trade partner with a total trade of US$33 billion and China's sixth largest investor with an accumulated total of US$28 billion. The two-way tourism has also thrived. In fact, Singapore has established itself as another gateway to China after Hong Kong.

At the political level, China and Singapore have continued to maintain a warm relationship, partly because there have been no outstanding issues and no areas of open conflict between the two countries. Following Deng Xiaoping's call to "learn from Singapore" in early 1992, China had organised numerous official "observation groups" to Singapore to study Singapore's development experiences. This culminated in the joint development of a large industrial park in Suzhou in 1994; the project eventually took off after overcoming initial hurdles.

Over the years, many top Chinese political and Party leaders, including virtually all the politburo members have visited Singapore. In return, most of Singapore's cabinet ministers and senior civil servants have also visited China to exchange views and strengthen ties.

Together with the rest of ASEAN, Singapore has developed a unique friendship with China, due to the strong cultural affinity and partly to Singapore's role as a useful and convenient conduit for China to interact politically and economically with other ASEAN countries. China also appreciates Singapore's one-China policy stand as well as its "special role" in contributing to cross-strait stability in her relations with Taiwan. Singapore, together with ASEAN, looks forward to many more good years of trade and development, positive cooperation, peace and mutual benefit with China.

China-ASEAN Economic Relations: Progress and Prospects

Liao Shaolian

The 24th ASEAN Ministerial Meeting attended by Chinese Foreign Minister Quan Qichen marked the beginning of official ties between China and the ASEAN grouping. By 1995, China had become a full dialogue partner of ASEAN and was the first dialogue partner to accede to the Treaty of Amity and Cooperation in Southeast Asia in October 2003. In the same year, ASEAN and China proclaimed a strategic partnership between them. The ASEAN-China Framework Agreement on Comprehensive Economic Cooperation, the first FTA between ASEAN and a dialogue partner, was signed in 2002 and provided for an ASEAN-China Free Trade Area (ACFTA) within a decade. Few people would have imagined that in only 16 years, the relationship was expanded to cover areas ranging from strategic and security partnership to political and economic cooperation as well as financial and socio-cultural exchanges.

Growing Bilateral Trade and Interdependency

Since 1991, bilateral trade between ASEAN and China has been growing rapidly reaching US$130.3 billion in 2005, which was more than 15 times the volume of 1991. The average annual growth rate in the last 15 years was more than 20 percent (around 40 percent in 2003 and 2004 respectively). According to the statistics from the ASEAN secretariat, ASEAN exports to China increased on average by over 46 percent a year from 2000 to reach US$52.4 billion in 2005. It was much higher than the annual growth rate of 4 percent in ASEAN exports to all markets besides China. With the rapid progress of bilateral trade, ASEAN and China have become important trading partners. Indeed, ASEAN's trade with China accounted for 4 percent of its total global trade in 2000 and 10.9 percent in 2005. China became ASEAN's third largest trading partner (after Japan and the European Union) in 2005 and ASEAN China's fifth largest (behind the US, the EU, Japan and Hong Kong Special Administrative Region).

A more detailed breakdown of exchanges between ASEAN and China reveals there is a significant growth in intra-industry trade, which indicates the structural change in commodity composition and closer economic linkages. For example, the share of parts and components in Malaysia's manufacturing exports to China rose from 6 percent in 1992 to 16 percent in 1996 and to 50 percent in 2000. As for Thailand, the figures were 8 percent, 29 percent, and 54 percent respectively.[1] Economic data also shows an emerging trend of a division of labour in the region. This in turn has helped to further economic integration and complementary relations between ASEAN economies and boosted the production of the manufacturing sector of ASEAN countries. For example, the share of electronics equipment and parts in total ASEAN exports to China increased from 35 to 49 percent between 2000 and 2005, while resource-based exports were reduced from 32 to 28 percent during the same period.[2]

As labour-intensive manufactured goods produced by China and ASEAN covered a broad range of products with different capital-labour ratios, there is also certain specialisation within this spectrum of manufactured exports among the countries concerned. Aside from having such specialisation in their supply of manufactured goods to the rest of the world, China and ASEAN also trade with each other based on such specialisation. With developments in exploiting horizontal division of labour, the bilateral trade has gradually shown

---

[1]Premachandra Athukorala, "Product Fragmentation and Trade Patterns in East Asia", Australian National University (Canberra), Division of Economics, Research School of Pacific and Asian Studies, *Working Papers in Trade and Development 2003/21* (2003), Table A2, p. 48.

[2]Such as fuels, edible oils, rubber, and forestry and mineral products.

complementarities within manufacturing industries. The products in machinery, transport and equipment industries dominate the bilateral trade in more recent years making intra-industry division of labour the basis for bilateral exchanges.[3] At the same time, niche products are being explored and identified for more exchanges. It can be expected that machinery and electronic products as well as high-tech products will account for increasingly larger proportions of China's export to ASEAN. Meanwhile, China's import of these two categories from ASEAN, especially old ASEAN members, will also increase by a large margin. This shows clearly that the diversity of manufactured products makes trade expansion possible despite similar export profiles and, intra-industry trade will continue to be a major part of China-ASEAN trade. Identification of trade niches will be the key factor in determining trade volumes and developing a new pattern of specialisation.

Increasing Investment and Other Fields of Cooperation

The past decade witnessed the rise of big Chinese transnational corporations investing overseas. In recent years, however, a large number of private Chinese companies are following this trend. The Chinese government has also adopted a series of decentralisation measures to encourage and support overseas investment. In fact, 12 provinces and cities have been authorised to approve overseas investment applications and to issue business certificates. Now investment in only seven countries (US, Japan, Singapore, North Korea, Pakistan, Israel and Iraq) is subject to approval from the Ministry of Commerce.

To further encourage overseas investments, China has signed an Agreement on Avoidance of Double Taxation with most of the ASEAN countries and the Bilateral Agreement on Investment Protection with all the ASEAN countries. It can be expected that more Chinese capital will be invested abroad and ASEAN will definitely be one of the major destinations of capital outflow. Both Asean-6 and Asean-4 will likely host much larger FDI from China, for example, in natural resources

---

[3]Ellen Palanca, "China's Changing Trade Patterns: Implications for ASEAN-China Trade," *PASCN Discussion Paper No. 99-20*, Ateneo de Manila University, July 1999.

development, manufacturing for the home and export markets, and tourism-related facilities. Some relocation of export-oriented, labour-intensive manufacturing activities from China to ASEAN can be anticipated as well. At the present, ASEAN's direct investment in China exceeds China's investment in ASEAN. By the end of 2005, ASEAN's accumulative investment amounted to US$38.5 billion, while China's accumulative investment was about US$1.2 billion.[4] China's direct investment in ASEAN is modest but it is growing steadily. For example, between 2003 and 2004, it registered an annual growth of US$210 million. However, with more and more Chinese companies investing in ASEAN, the capital flow will become a bit more balanced in the future.

Besides trade and direct investment, further progress in cooperation can be seen in other areas such as culture, arts and educational, youth and other people-to-people exchanges. In 2005, ASEAN hosted three million tourists from China, or just 6 percent of the total of 51.3 million arrivals. According to the World Tourism Organisation, out-bound tourists from China would reach 100 million by 2020. ASEAN's well-developed and diversified tourism sector should be able to cater for a much larger slice of this huge market.

Implications of CAFTA on Future China-ASEAN Relations

Looking to the future, there is still a lot of room for China-ASEAN economic relations to progress. China's trade with each ASEAN country is still relatively small even though China's trade with ASEAN as a whole is growing rapidly. This indicates that there is great potential for further expansion of bilateral trade. Furthermore, during the period of slow growth in many developed countries, China can serve as an alternative market for ASEAN exports. This trend will help offset declining market share elsewhere, especially during the present period of economic recovery and high growth. More importantly, China's continuing high economic growth, together with its accession to the World Trade Organisation in 2001, implies even bigger import potentials. Furthermore, it is expected that its demand for better quality

---

[4]*International Business Daily*, 11 July 2006.

and a greater variety of consumer goods will rise as its per capita income increases. In addition, China is also increasing its imports on commodity products such as oil, rubber, palm oil and wood products to fuel its rapid industrialisation process. China's growth will also induce a further expansion of imports of capital goods and intermediate goods, which means that the share of machinery, electronic and high-tech products in its bilateral trade with ASEAN will increase further.

As for the implementation of trade liberalisation within the framework of China-ASEAN Free Trade Area (CAFTA), since China is fulfilling its market opening commitments to the WTO,[5] it will not take as long as ten years, as described in the Framework Agreement, to liberalise most of the commodities in its trade with ASEAN.

Bilateral trade between China and ASEAN countries is also expected to grow as both sides have concluded an agreement on trade in goods and one on a dispute-settlement mechanism in 2004. Now they are working on an agreement on trade in services and one on investment. They are also cooperating in other areas such as agriculture, information and communications technology (ICT), transportation, energy, public health, culture and tourism, and in the development of the Mekong Basin.

More importantly, the lifting of tax barriers as a result of CAFTA will increase the region's market appeal and further attract regional and non-regional FDI that seek to tap the potential of new markets. As the intra-regional flow of capital and commodities is becoming more convenient, firms will be able to break up the value chain by distributing production stages throughout the region in a way that exploits the individual members' comparative advantages. Besides, subsidiaries will be able to enjoy greater economies of scale, thus making them more profitable. Transnational businesses investing in ASEAN will also enjoy lower tariffs when exploring markets in China. Furthermore, China is now opening to foreign investors sectors such as commerce, foreign trade, banking, insurance, securities, telecommunications, tourism and

---

[5]According to the commitments made by China during its negotiations with WTO members in ASEAN, China promised to lower its tariffs for ASEAN products by 34–47 percent in five years, much faster than the tariff reduction of the country as a whole. (*International Economic Cooperation*, 2003, No. 6, p. 55)

media services. This means that more ASEAN business people will come to invest in these newly opened sectors.

Though there is great potential for closer economic cooperation in the future, the countries concerned will also have to face various challenges. Increased competition in home and third-country markets can be expected and will encourage both sides to make necessary adjustments so as to increase productivity and competitiveness of their products. As their relationship continues to grow closer, more and more cooperation mechanisms will be established. From a long-term perspective, it is important that both sides exert greater efforts to expand mutual trust and define the norms that will guide their political, security as well as economic relations. In order to further enhance economic complementarities, it is essential to engage in in-depth study so as to promote mutual understanding and continuously search for new fields and ways of economic and technological cooperation.

Malaysia-China Relations: Looking Beyond Fears and Inadequacies

Stephen Leong

Malaysia-China relation today is a tale of how two countries have successfully transformed a negative relationship into a mutually beneficial partnership. After Malaysia gained independence from Great Britain in 1957, and until 1971 when she voted for Beijing's entry into the United Nations to replace the Republic of China, ties between the two countries were strained because of a clash of ideologies. Adversely affected by its own communist insurrection (1948–60), Malaysia was very much against Communism. China's support for the Malayan Communist Party and its refusal to recognise Malaysia's formation in 1965, and the upheaval in China during the Cultural Revolution were major obstacles to the normalisation of relations.[1]

The turning point in bilateral relations came in 1971 when then Malaysian Prime Minister Tun Abdul Razak fervently sought to promote ASEAN's Zone of Peace, Freedom and Neutrality (ZOPFAN). He believed that for ZOPFAN to succeed, it was necessary for ASEAN to come to terms with China. The Malaysian leader already foresaw that China's emergence as a major regional power in the years ahead would heavily impact on its neighbours.[2]

---

[1]Stephen Leong, "Malaysia and the People's Republic of China in the 1980s: Political Vigilance and Economic Pragmatism," *Asian Survey*, Vol. XXVI, No. 10, October 1987; Lee Poh Ping and Lee Kam Hing, "Malaysia-China Relations: A Review," paper presented at International Conference on Emerging China: Implications and Challenges for Southeast Asia, Kuala Lumpur, 22–23 July 2004, pp. 3–5.

[2]Mohd Najib Abdul Razak, *Globalising Malaysia: Towards Building A Developed Nation*. Kuala Lumpur: MPH Publications, 2006, pp. 129–137.

Like other ASEAN members, Malaysia could have accepted the status quo in inter-state relations with Communist China and non-Communist ASEAN countries going their own paths. It would seem fine if the paths do not clash with each other, but there was no assurance that they would not. Clearly, it would be far better if a seemingly no-win situation could be creatively transformed into a mutually beneficial win-win relationship with both sides cooperating with one another for a brighter future in the region.[3]

Interestingly, in 1971, Malaysia's new approach to China was quite similar to that of China's then arch enemy, the United States. The anti-Communist Nixon Administration had adopted bold steps to come to terms with Beijing. As in the case of US ping-pong diplomacy, Malaysia's badminton diplomacy quickly led it to vote for Beijing's entry into the UN by the end of the year. In 1974, Prime Minister Tun Abdul Razak with a large Malaysian contingent visited Beijing and signed an agreement for establishing diplomatic relations with China. Malaysia's path-breaking act led the Philippines and Thailand to establish official ties with China in 1975. Soon, other members of ASEAN followed suit.[4]

So did Malaysia view China as a threat? Until the last years of the Mao Zedong era, there was no doubt that Malaysia saw China as a threat. However, with Mao's demise in 1976 and China's open-door policy under Deng Xiaoping from 1978, Malaysia and China began to develop closer bilateral relations.[5]

A big boost in Kuala Lumpur-Beijing relations occurred at the end of 1990, when Chinese Premier Li Peng visited Malaysia. Prime Minister Mahathir Mohamed's proposal to set up an East Asian Economic Group had the support of China.[6]

Meanwhile, economic relations were also enhanced substantially. Bilateral trade grew from US$160 million (RM569.60 million) in 1974

---

[3]Ibid., pp. 134–136.

[4]Ibid., p. 140.

[5]Ibid., p. 141.

[6]"China-Malaysia Relations: Challenges and Opportunities in the 21st Century," speech by Dr Mahathir Mohamed, Prime Minister of Malaysia, at 3rd Malaysia-China Forum, Beijing, 19 August 1999, p. 6; "Building the East Asian Community," speech by Dr Mahathir Mohamed, Prime Minister of Malaysia at First East Asia Congress, Kuala Lumpur, 4 August 2003, p. 1.

to US$30.7 billion (RM109.29 billion) in October 2006; the figure was expected to hit US$36 billion by the end of 2006.[7] For some years now, China has been a major buyer of Malaysian palm oil. In 2005, it purchased about three million tonnes of Malaysian crude palm oil worth US$1.2 billion, representing 75 percent of all palm oil imported by China.[8] In 2005, Malaysia's investment in China totalled US$247.03 million (RM914 million) while Chinese investment in Malaysia was US$19.7 million (RM73 million).[9] Malaysia has also been targeting China as a huge tourism market. In 2005 Chinese tourist arrivals totalled 350,000 and 420,000 were expected for 2006 representing a 20 percent year-on-year increase.[10]

Like many other countries in the region, Malaysia has greatly benefitted from China's spectacular economic growth. While China is undoubtedly a great competitor or challenger in the economic arena, Kuala Lumpur, at the same time, regards it as a vast opportunity.[11]

Neither does Malaysia view China as a threat in the political-security arena. Kuala Lumpur has been encouraged by both Beijing's initiatives to promote better bilateral relations as well as improve its ties with other ASEAN countries. China's decision not to devalue the yuan during the Asian financial crisis, its proposal for an ASEAN-China Free Trade Agreement, the signing of the Declaration of Conduct in the South China Sea with ASEAN, its accession to the Treaty of Amity and Cooperation, its agreement with ASEAN members for a strategic partnership for peace and prosperity, and most recently its announcement of its intention to sign the Southeast Asia Nuclear Weapons Free Zone Treaty have all demonstrated China's desire to cooperate with its ASEAN neighbours in promoting peace and

---

[7]*New Straits Times*, 9 December 2006, p. 54.

[8]"China Firms Seek Malaysian Palm Oil Waste for Biodiesel," *Bernama.com*, 19 June 2006.

[9]Central Bank Malaysia, *Monthly Statistics Bulletin*, September 2006, p. 137.

[10]"Malaysia Attaches Importance to Tourism Market in China," *China View*, 13 December 2006, p. 1.

[11]"China — A Challenge or An Opportunity for Asia?" speech by Dr Mahathir Mohamed, Prime Minister of Malaysia at 8th Nikkei Conference on the Future of Asia, Tokyo, 21 May 2002.

prosperity for the region.[12] Also, in the last few years, together with ASEAN countries and its two Northeast Asian neighbours Japan and Korea, China has participated in the ASEAN Plus Three process, the unprecedented regional enterprise to build an East Asian Community.

Right from Malaysia's independence in 1957, Malaysia-China relations have clearly been transformed from one of distrust, even hostility, to one of growing trust and friendship. Malaysian Prime Minister Abdullah Badawi's statement at the China-Malaysia Economic Conference in Kuala Lumpur in 2004 clearly showed Malaysia's stance: "Our China policy showed that if you can look beyond your fears and inadequacies, and can think and act from principled positions, rewards will follow."[13]

It is true that while bilateral relations with its giant neighbour up north have greatly improved over the years, still some may wish to remind Kuala Lumpur of future uncertainties (especially stemming from China's military buildup and possible use of force to settle the dispute over territorial claims in the South China Sea).[14] While these important issues could negatively affect regional peace and stability, Malaysia nevertheless feels that as dialogue and consultation have so positively reduced tensions on both sides in the last two decades, a continuation of this strategy can further enhance trust and friendship between ASEAN members and China, along with efforts by China's Northeast Asian neighbours Korea and Japan.

Finally, while Malaysia and China have mutually benefitted from closer bilateral relations, to attain enduring peace for the region, the ASEAN Plus Three process of regional community building would be the best way forward.[15]

---

[12]*ASEAN-CHINA Dialogue Relations, 15th Anniversary Commemorative Magazine.* Jakarta: ASEAN Secretariat, 2006, pp. 5–6.

[13]"Keynote Address," by Abdullah Haji Ahmad Badawi, Prime Minister of Malaysia at China-Malaysia Economic Conference 2004, Kuala Lumpur, 24 February 2004.

[14]Herbert Yee and Ian Story, *The China Threat: Perceptions, Myths and Reality.* London: Routledge and Curzon, 2002; Marvin C. Ott, "Southeast Asian Security Challenges: America's Response?" *Strategic Forum,* No. 222, October 2006, p. 5.

[15]Stephen Leong, "East Asian Vision Taking Shape," *The Star,* 12 December 2005.

Philippines-China Relations: "Golden Age of Partnership"

Ellen Palanca

The cooperation between the Philippines and China has accelerated very quickly in the last few years. The relations have been described by both sides as having reached the "golden age of partnership". Philippines-China relations have come a long way. Just a few years ago, Filipinos still perceived China as a threat, both to Philippine national security and its economy. Today such perceptions do not seem to exist anymore among Filipinos.

Exchange of High-Level Visits

There has been an intensification of high-level visits between China and Philippines in the last few years. Philippine President Gloria Macapagal Arroyo made a state visit in October 2003 to China. The visit was reciprocated by Chinese President Hu Jintao in April 2005. In October 2006, Mrs. Arroyo, as the rotating president of ASEAN, also attended the China-ASEAN Investment and Business Summit in Nanning where she was met by Premier Wen Jiabao. From there, she visited two more provinces: Fujian and Jiangxi. In January 2007 Premier Wen made a state visit to the Philippines after the East Asian Summit there.

Security Cooperation

A very significant development in China's cooperation with ASEAN countries is its multi-faceted nature. It goes beyond the usual economic and cultural dimensions, and has extended to security and defence cooperation, as well as development projects.

The defence and security cooperation with the Philippines is increasingly gaining significance in the Philippines-China relations and it is an important confidence building measure. Although the magnitude of the Philippines' defence cooperation with China is small compared with its cooperation with the US, it is nevertheless a milestone in Philippines' foreign relations considering their hostility during the Cold War and more recently, the disputes they had over the Spratley territories. Recently, the two sides launched a mechanism for defence and security consultations to boost cooperation in this area. In addition, China donated RMB10 billion in 2004 and 2005 for some engineering and medical needs of the Armed Forces of the Philippines. Problems of terrorism and transnational crimes are also areas of military cooperation between the two countries.

The issue of South China Sea territorial claim has been shelved with the signing in 2002 of the Declaration on the Conduct of Parties in the South China Sea, with the provision that no territorial sovereignty claim can be made by any party and also that no improvement on the territories can be made by any party. Since then joint activities on confidence building have been undertaken. China, the Philippines and Vietnam have jointly undertaken a project to survey an area there using scientific research methods.

Philippines-China Bilateral Trade

Trade reached almost US$5 billion in 2005, with the Philippines enjoying a surplus of close to US$1 billion. For 1993, the trade value was just around US$350 million. Until 2001, the Philippines had an annual trade deficit with China. The share of trade with China also grew significantly, from 1–2 percent in the early 1990s to almost 6–8 percent since 2000. This means that the rate of growth is greater for Philippines' trade with China than for its trade with the rest of the world.

However, there is a loss of diversification in the Philippine exports to China. For 2005, more than 80 percent of exports were electronics products. The Philippines provides intermediate inputs for final IT products made in China (see Tables 1–4).

Table 1. Philippine Exports to China, Selected Years (FOB Value in Million US$)

Year	Exports to China	% Share in Total Exports
1993	173.87	1.53
1998	343.68	1.17
2002	1,352.90	3.86
2005	2,728.06	10.30

Table 2. Philippine Imports from China, Selected Years (FOB Value in Million US$)

Year	Imports to China	% Share in Total Imports
1993	180.66	1.03
1998	1,198.89	4.04
2002	1,231.19	3.68
2005	1,912.06	6.22

Table 3. Merchandise Exports to China, Selected Years, by Major Product Grouping (% of Total Exports)

Major Product Grouping	1998 % Share	2002 % Share	2005 % Share
Consumer Manufactures	2.14	1.33	0.58
Food and Food Preparations	11.82	2.85	0.80
Resource-Based Products	51.20	15.46	8.53
Industrial Manufactures	28.63	72.47	88.81
Special Transactions	6.21	7.89	1.28

Table 4. Merchandise Imports from China, Selected Years, by Major Product Grouping (% of Total Imports)

Major Product Grouping	1998 % Share	2002 % Share	2005 % Share
Consumer Manufactures	5.39	9.85	5.64
Food and Food Preparations	39.54	8.69	3.29
Resource-Based Products	14.94	22.92	15.50
Industrial Manufactures	39.82	57.64	73.72
Special Transactions	0.32	0.90	1.85

Investments and Development Assistance

The high-level official dialogues have generated many official investments and assistance from China. The increase was particularly sharp in 2006. According to Philippine official figures, Chinese investments in the Philippines grew from US$3.8 million in 2005 to US$322 million in 2006, due to the infusion of capital in several development projects. In June 2006, at a Forum on Comprehensive Economic Cooperation held in the Philippines, trade ministers from both sides signed a Memorandum Of Understanding to cooperate in almost all economic sectors: tourism, agriculture, fisheries, mining, infrastructure and mass housing. China committed US$32 billion for this cooperation.

As the fastest growing economy in the world with a focus on manufacturing, China's demand for raw materials has surged, mopping up natural resources in many developing countries. China is also losing its comparative advantage in agricultural products for which it has technological expertise. In its investment cooperation with the Philippines, agriculture, fishery and mining are among the areas of cooperation. In the case of agriculture, one million hectares of land will be used to plant hybrid rice, corn and sorghum, and 10 thousand fish cages will be built for the cultivation of marine products. Products from such agricultural and fishery activities are for export to China eventually.

For agricultural cooperation, China has introduced hybrid rice and hybrid corn, and provided technological assistance to Philippine farmers. For these, the Philippine-Sino Center for Agricultural Technology funded by China was set up in 2003. For mining, there is already a deal between China's nickel giant, the Jinchuan Group, which supplies 90 percent of China's nickel, and Philnico Industrial Corporation, which owns the rights to the largest nickel deposit in the Philippines. The Chinese nickel firm is to buy a 15 percent stake in Philnico for US$45 million.

Mining is a controversial topic in the Philippines. Although mining projects were studied by the Department of Environment and Natural Resources before approval was granted, many environmental groups are still concerned about the negative effects on the environment. Moreover,

China's mining history has not been a rosy one. It has been proposed that China can contribute capital to the development of the industry if a safer and more sophisticated mining technology has been adopted — one that ensures safety and less environmental damage.

China focuses on infrastructure construction in its development assistance for the Philippines. The largest Chinese development project in the Philippines so far is the construction of railroads: a North Rail going north of Manila and a South Rail which goes to the south. This project is to be built by the China National Machinery and Engineering Group, one of China's top 10 enterprises. A concession loan of US$900 million has been committed by China for this project: US$500 million is for the railroad project and US$400 million for the construction of housing units for those affected by the railroad construction. The housing project aims to build one million housing units in the next five years. As it is a government project that involves large sums of money, for a while, it attracted the attention of opposition politicians who questioned the government's decision and technical competency of the Chinese company. The controversies have since been resolved.

Tourism and People-to-People Contact

Tourism between the two countries has also improved. In general, Filipino tourists to China far exceed Chinese tourists to the Philippines. However, recent Chinese tourist arrivals had nearly tripled from 39,581 in 2004 to 107,456 in 2005 when the Philippines allowed the procurement of visa upon arrival.[1]

Besides tourism, Philippines and China are also putting more emphasis on people-to-people interactions to promote harmony and mutual understanding. With respect to promoting economic cooperation between China and ASEAN through people-to-people contacts, the Nanning Expo has been very successful. Another venue for such contacts is the Confucius Institutes, i.e., a global chain of Chinese

---

[1]"New Record for Chinese Tourist Arrivals in RP," posted at http://www. goodnewspilipinas.com/docs/beauty_of_the_philippines/archived/record_chinese_ tourist.html, accessed on 9 May 2007.

cultural centres which is growing extremely quickly. Philippines has one Confucian Institute at the Ateneo de Manila University.

Existing Issues in Philippines-China Relations

In sum, Philippines-China relations have significantly improved, and China is no longer viewed as a threat in the Philippines. Furthermore, both nations have benefitted from growing trade, investment, and tourism. Nevertheless, there are still areas where cooperation can be advanced and frictions avoided. In the area of trade, Philippine exports to China are too concentrated on electronics products and primary resources. Cooperation between businessmen of both countries can lead to new trade niches for the Philippines in China. Moreover, Chinese investments in Philippine manufacturing can help upgrade Philippines technology and produce innovative products which can improve the Philippine export profile.

On the social front, Philippine-China relations are adversely affected by the illegal activities committed by Chinese nationals in kidnapping, drug-pushing and drug-manufacturing, and fishing and poaching on Philippine seas. Frictions develop whenever the Chinese Embassy in Manila intercedes and requests for the release of the illegal fishermen and poachers, despite the two countries' commitment to solve transnational crimes.

Managing China-Philippines Relations Through Dialogue

Shen Hongfang

China-Philippines bilateral relations is at an all time high and this is ascribed mostly to the frequent multi-level dialogues and contacts between the two sides. These mechanisms, which are marked by regular official visits and people-to-people exchanges, allowed the Philippine government and the public to recognise the benefits of peaceful co-existence and the positive effects of China's phenomenal economic growth.[1] Today, China-Philippines cooperation not only covers the areas of trade and investment, but also other fields, including tourism, agriculture, fisheries, infrastructure construction and mineral resources exploitations, military and defence, judicial assistance, drug control and transnational crimes.[2] China-Philippines bilateral relations would not have reached this level if both sides did not take appropriate steps to resolve outstanding differences that persisted throughout and after the Cold War. This paper traces how China and the Philippines were able work out these differences to forge a strong and lasting partnership.

---

[1] Various consultation and cooperation mechanisms have been established including the foreign ministry consultations, consular consultations, the Joint Trade Committee, the Joint Committee on Agriculture and the Joint Committee on Science and Technology.

[2] For concrete economic projects of bilateral cooperation in recently years, see Shen Hongfang, "Sino-Philippine Relations in the Context of China-ASEAN Free trade Agreement," *EAI Working paper No. 118*, 30 June 2005, National University of Singapore; Charissa M. Luci, "Bilateral Ties with China at an All-time High," Philippine English Newspaper *Mania Bulletin*, 28 October 2006.

Overcoming Differences

One of the major problems in China-Philippines relations was trade imbalance. Philippines has been suffering from deficits in its trade with China since the establishment of diplomatic relations in 1975. This generated complaints in the Philippines that trade deficits with China had caused the bankruptcy of many small and medium export enterprises and unemployment in the country. Aware of these negative sentiments in the Philippines, Beijing introduced various measures to increase Philippine exports to China markets. As a result, Philippine exports to China expanded from US$130 million in 1991 to US$13 billion in 2005, registering a 99-fold increase. More importantly, Philippine-China trade balance was transformed from a trade deficit of US$1.23 billion in 1991 to a trade surplus of US$8.1 billion for the Philipppines in 2005. At the same time, from 1991 to 2005, China-Philippines bilateral trade increased more than 45-fold from US$385 million in 1991 to US$17.6 billion in 2005.

The reversal of China-Philippines trade status has profound effects on the Philippine economy as it brought many business opportunities for many enterprises in the country, which in turn, created jobs for the people. The growing trade between China and the Philippines also brought in huge volumes of cheap but relatively high quality Chinese goods welcomed by the Philippine lower and medium class.[3] This development was acknowledged by both the government and the public, thus paving the way for better China-Philippines relations.

A second problem that both sides are working hard to overcome is to dismiss the "China threat" theory that was partly a Cold War legacy and partly due to fears of China's economic boom and a massive FDI inflow. One way is to conduct regular official contacts and people-to-people exchanges. Furthermore, the Philippine leadership has repeatedly pronounced its view that a rising China is beneficial to the country and the region. For instance, President Gloria Arroyo announced during her visit to China in October 2006 that the attractiveness of China to Western investments will benefit ASEAN because Chinese companies

---

[3]*Manila Bulletin*, 31 October 2006

will bring their excess capital to the region.[4] In addition, during a closed-door bilateral meeting with Chinese Premier Wen Jiabao, Arroyo hailed China's economic strength and increasing ties as a boon for Southeast Asia. She said, "China has surged on the world stage and ASEAN has surged with it".[5] Such expressions suggest that Philippines' perception of China has changed dramatically, especially in light of a view formerly subscribed by the Philippine government that the shortage of the nation's FDI is due to "the improper way of the Chinese government in absorbing foreign investment". In turn, this change has broadened the view of Philippine officials and the public towards China-Philippines relations. Guided by this new vision, at China and ASEAN trade and economic ministers meeting held in Cebu, the Philippines, on 8 December 2006, the Philippines abandoned its formerly negative view towards the China-ASEAN FTA (CAFTA) and finally approved an Early Harvest Programme between China and the Philippines. This programme was included in the 2nd Amendment Protocol under the framework of the CAFTA.[6] Approval of the agreement will no doubt facilitate the implementation of China-ASEAN Agreements on Trade in Goods as well as the formulation of the CAFTA.

Another persisting problem that is hindering China-Philippines relations is the territorial disputes in the South China Sea. However, through multilateral and bilateral dialogues and negotiations and other "confident-building activities", China, Philippines and other involved parties were able to sidestep the disputes and turn the flash spot into peaceful water. With the support of the Philippines and Chinese leadership, joint exploration in the South China Sea is gaining momentum. For instance, in September 2004, when President Arroyo visited China, an agreement of Joint Marine Seismic Undertaking was signed between China National Offshore Oil Company and

---

[4]*Manila Bulletin*, 27 October 2006

[5]*Manila Bulletin*, 31 October 2006

[6]The other two agreements were the amendment of special goods list in China-Indonesia Early Harvest Programme and China-Vietnam Agreements on Trade in Goods. From Network Centre of MOFCOM, Supplement Agreement on China-ASEAN FTA Signed. http://english.mofcom.gov.cn/newsrelease/significantnews/200612/200612 04009381.html.

Philippine's National Oil Company to conduct a three-year joint study on oil exploration in the South China Sea. Both sides are confident that conducive joint ventures like these could help maintain peace and stability in the South China Sea, which would in turn enhance mutual trust and cooperation between the claiming countries.[7]

What to Expect in the Future

China-Philippines relation is likely to continue to grow as the CAFTA takes gradual effect. As stated by President Arroyo, China is in the position to take the lead in promoting good neighbourly relations and regional cooperation in a spirit of equality, respect, consultation and mutual benefits and through the establishment of the CAFTA in 2010.[8]

---

[7]"Premier Wen Jiabao's Speech at China-ASEAN Summit," *China Daily*, 30 October 2006.

[8]*Manila Bulletin*, 31 October 2006.

Roundtable Discussion on ASEAN-China Relations ?

By Participants of the Symposium of "ASEAN-China Relations: Harmony and Development" Singapore, 18 December 2006

Compiled by Lim Tin Seng, Tan Soon Heng, Teng Siow Song and Zheng Yi

Prof. Koh began the Roundtable session by inviting Mr. Jusuf Wanandi and Mr. Khamphan Simmalavong to give a five-minute speech before opening up the floor for questions.

Mr. Wanandi stated that along with the many benefits of maturing ASEAN-China relations, there are also a lot of challenges. First, the issue of territorial disputes in the South China Sea has yet to be solved. Apart from signing the Declaration on the Conduct of Parties in the South China Sea in 2002, China will do well to help strengthen the declaration and settle the existing disputes. Second, ASEAN and China must look beyond the relationship to include other important countries such as the United States, Russia, Australia and New Zealand to keep the partnership in balance. Third, dialogues on domestic development are an important aspect in ASEAN-China relationship as fast economic development must also be accompanied by fast political development. To do this, China and ASEAN should work together through various means such as Track Two dialogues to learn from each other. Fourth, though ASEAN-China economic relations are not a zero-sum game, certain competition is good as it will lead to innovation and improvement. Finally, cultural and people-to-people exchanges should not be left out in ASEAN-China partnership. Mr. Wanandi also urged China to look into its environmental problems more responsively, especially on the Mekong River.

To Mr. Simmalavong, ASEAN-China relationship has three main pillars: 1) security and political cooperation, 2) economic cooperation and 3) social cooperation. Many agreements such as the Declaration on the Conduct of Parties in the South China Sea, Southeast Asia Nuclear Weapon Free Zone and CAFTA are crafted based on the above. The strengthening of ASEAN-China cooperation will bring about many benefits such as narrowing the development gap in ASEAN. ASEAN and China should work together to enhance cooperation and resolve standing disputes to prevent the escalation of disputes into an armed conflict. Mr. Simmalavong hopes that ASEAN and China will continue to foster good mutual relations and bring prosperity to the region.

To Mr Wanandi's comments, Prof. Wang Yan said that China views the territorial disputes in the South China Sea as a great challenge. She also said that such issues will need a lot of time and patience to resolve and China has the patience and wisdom to do so. Prof. Wang also added that China will abide by the Declaration on the Conduct of Parties in the South China Sea.

Dr. Ignatius Wibowo Wibisono commented that CAFTA will not necessarily bring closer cooperation between ASEAN and China. He noted that the North America Free Trade Agreement (NAFTA) has caused many disagreements and unfair treatment among the nations involved, particularly Mexico. Dr. Wibowo cited that CAFTA has led to a flood of Chinese goods in the region. According to him, this has disrupted the Indonesian market and created a great deal of pressure on Indonesian Small and Medium Enterprises (SMEs).

Prof. Koh's response to this is, there is bound to be competition with or without a FTA. However, he added that such competition should not be seen as a zero sum game. A September 2006 World Bank report stated that 55 percent of the world's trade came from this region driven by the private sector and characterised by intra-regional trade. This is significant because it has given the region a production platform. Based on this, Prof. Koh believes that trade and competition here is actually a win-win situation.

Mr. Wanandi added that competition from China has actually prompted Indonesia to improve its industries and laws. Indonesian SMEs especially are being forced to improve their efficiency, while the government is compelled to improve its laws and regulations on trade and industries.

Dr. Sheng Lijun saw the need to have more people-to-people and cultural exchanges to strengthen China-ASEAN relationship and cohesiveness. He also said that these could actually be more effective than just high level exchanges.

To this, Dr Stephen Leong said that ASEAN and China have been working to promote ties using the social channel through tourism. He also said that investment from the private sector from ASEAN to China and vice versa is also facilitating these exchanges.

Prof. Liao echoed Dr. Sheng's suggestion for more people-to-people exchanges to raise the awareness of cooperation between ASEAN and China. He said that there are still many Chinese in the countryside who do not even know what CAFTA is. He also added that there should also be more cultural exchanges, particularly in arts.

Prof. Koh agreed with Prof. Liao that there is a need to have more exchanges between China and ASEAN on arts. He quoted the Director of the Chinese National Arts Museum in Beijing as saying that they had great difficulties preparing for the exhibition on the art history of ASEAN because they did not have access to ASEAN art.

Dr. Lai Hongyi suggested that the impact of trade could be viewed differently by different groups of the society. He explained that cheap Chinese textile exported to the United States for instance could please millions of consumers and at the same time affect the textile industries in the country. Dr. Lai also added that there should be more focus on the positive rather than the negative impact of China-ASEAN trade. He also raised the issue of whether China will become the main driver of ASEAN-China relations in the near future and asked about the implications if China is to become the main driver.

Prof. Koh responded by saying that it is better for ASEAN to be courted by China rather than not being courted at all. He also said that China's initiatives have led other nations such as Japan and the United States to step up their engagement with ASEAN. Prof. Koh then proceeded to invite each panellist to make a brief statement on ASEAN-China relations before calling the symposium to an end.

Prof. Wang Yan stated that China respects ASEAN way of doing things. She also said that China is stepping up efforts to increase and expand its youth exchange programmes between China and ASEAN and vice versa.

Prof. Wong stated that ASEAN-China relationship is very dynamic and it will become even more vibrant in the coming years.

Mr. Wanandi felt that the mutual engagement between ASEAN and China is good and will only lead to a more sophisticated and elaborate relationship.

Mr. Simmalavong said that the spirit of cooperation and peaceful development between ASEAN and China should continue.

Dr. Stephen Leong stated that since the world will be watching how ASEAN-China relationship will be developing in the coming years, it will be a good opportunity to display the importance of the partnership.

Prof. Liao revisited the "harmony and development" theme and stated that the word "development" has a deeper meaning to it than just growth. Therefore, he urged the others not to misinterpret the term.

Prof. Koh made his final statement saying that aside from robust economic growth and development in China and ASEAN, it is important that the environment should not be ignored. He concluded that the term "harmony" should therefore include not only international and people-to-people relations but also the environment.

Prof. Wong closed the symposium by thanking the participants and announcing that the East Asian Institute will be publishing the materials presented in the symposium into a monograph.

Index